The Age
Beautifully
Cookbook

The Age Beautifully Cookbook

Easy and Exotic Longevity Secrets from Around the World

Grace O

creator of FOODTRIENTS

Foreword by Kathy Van Ness

Skyhorse Publishing

Visit our website at www.skyhorsepublishing.com.

10 9 8 7 6 5 4 3 2 1

Library of Congress Cataloging-in-Publication Data is available on file.

FoodTrients® Board of Advisors
Andre Berger, MD
John M. Kennedy, MD
Zein Obagi, MD
Mao Shing Ni, PhD, DOM, ABAAHP, L.Ac.
Monica Reinagel, MS, LN, CNS
Mark A. Rosenberg, MD

Publishing Team
Executive Editor: Barbara Weller, Broadthink
Editor: Shelly Kale
Designer: Lynn Fleschutz
Photos by Matthew Fried, unless otherwise noted
Contributing writer: Angela Pettera
Editorial assistant: Emily Hunt
Publishing consultants: Nancy Cushing-Jones, Cynthia Cleveland,
and Barbara Weller, Broadthink
Nutrition consultant: Monica Reinagel, MS, LN, CNS

Cover design by Lynn Fleschutz
Cover photo credit: Matthew Fried

Print ISBN: 978-1-63450-797-4
Ebook ISBN: 978-1-63450-803-2

Printed in China

The recipes and information in this book do not replace advice from a doctor or qualified health practitioner. Always consult your health practitioner before changing any routine to your lifestyle, including diet and exercise. The author and publisher disclaim all responsibility for any loss or liability incurred as a result of using this book.

Contents

Contents

Main Courses continued

Contents

Part 3: RESOURCES

Acknowledgments

As with my first FoodTrients® cookbook, with much love and appreciation I dedicate this book to my parents, whose work in the fields of nutrition, medicine, and the culinary arts ignited my lifelong passion for cooking with both healthful and tasty ingredients; to my husband Rupert, whose endless support helps sustain me in life and in my kitchen as I test my recipes; and to Nancy O'Connor, in whose loving memory I continue to find strength, comfort, and common-sense guidance.

Many exceptional people have contributed to the development and publication of this book. I cannot thank enough, from the bottom of my heart, my expert food preparation and test-kitchen team: Angie Abrantes Fischer, Jean Paul Dellosa, Osita Forral, and Genevieve Valarao; my dedicated book development team: writer, researcher, and photo stylist Angela Pettera, executive editor Barbara Weller, and cookbook editor Shelly Kale; and my inspirational design and production team: photographer Matthew Fried and book and cover designer Lynn Fleschutz. I also want to thank nutritionist and author Monica Reinagel, MS, LN, CNS, for her wonderful work reviewing, editing, and advising us on every recipe in this book.

The following friends and colleagues each contributed one recipe to this cookbook, so I want to thank Dr. Lynn Blair, Carmencita Juco, and Robb Weller.

Finally, I am thankful every day for my steadfast FoodTrients consultants: Broadthink principals Cynthia Cleveland, Nancy Cushing-Jones, and Barbara Weller, who, among many other initiatives, have introduced me to my wonderful publisher, Skyhorse.

Foreword

I first became acquainted with Grace O and her work combining nutritionally beneficial foods with wonderfully tasty recipes through her cookbook *The Age GRACEfully Cookbook: The Power of FoodTrients to Promote Health and Well-Being for a Joyful and Sustainable Life.*

Both FoodTrients® and the Golden Door have complementary passions and purposes regarding how to live a nutritious life. Both originally were rooted in Asian culture and now have expanded to include the best ingredients and influences from around the world. The Golden Door's philosophy is based on the belief that beauty begins from within. We pride ourselves on being one of the first spas to create cuisine that is both nutritious, artfully presented, and layered with flavors. We see a similar vision in Grace O's innovative fusion of international and American flavors, familiar and exotic ingredients, and specific nutrients that fight disease and the wear and tear of aging.

Over the past three decades, my career has involved working with several different fashion and luxury brands and businesses—all focused on defining and delivering "beautiful" products. Now, as the General Manager of the premiere luxury spa in America, I am always looking for ways to enhance beauty from within first. In addition to our own extensive gardens, our food-sourcing relationships are with local farmers, fishermen, and ranchers. Our Executive Chef Greg Frey and his staff are delighted to explore Grace O's recipes for the Golden Door because she is focused on providing recipes that have also been vetted by a nationally recognized nutritionist, Monica Reinagel.

The Golden Door also cares about what we put in our bodies. With the right care, each of us has the potential to age beautifully! The Golden Door has a long history as the spa where Hollywood stars like Elizabeth Taylor and Burt Lancaster would visit to shape up in-between film roles. In more recent times, we have welcomed famous visitors like Oprah Winfrey and Martha Stewart. Everyone comes not only for the fitness and the various beauty treatments, but also for our delicious and rejuvenating spa cuisine. Recently, the Golden Door expanded its grounds to include five biodynamic culinary, floral, and herb gardens.

Being conscious of what you eat is a critical first step to aging beautifully. Grace O understands how critical this first step is and we are therefore delighted to support FoodTrients at the Golden Door.

With *The Age Beautifully Cookbook,* Grace O provides a tasty roadmap for promoting beautiful skin, lustrous hair, strong bones, free-flowing arteries, and a vibrant mind.

Kathy Van Ness
General Manager, The Golden Door Spa, goldendoor.com

part 1

AGE BEAUTIFULLY WITH FOODTRIENTS®

Introduction

As I've been telling my story these past few years about how I developed an anti-aging cookbook based on the food-is-medicine principle, I've expanded my method for creating delicious, comforting recipes designed to keep you young, healthy, and beautiful.

That's the focus of the *Age Beautifully Cookbook: Easy and Exotic Longevity Secrets from Around the World.* The recipes are mainly quick and easy to make and will introduce readers to age-defying foods and flavors from around the world—with a particular emphasis on beauty that emanates from the inside. As I have said many times, even the most expensive creams on the market can't do as much for your health as feeding your body the right nutrients.

The most beautiful people I know are not model perfect. They're people who wear a gorgeous smile along with their glowing skin, bright eyes, healthy body, and positive energy. They look good because they feel good. But eating well doesn't mean sacrificing the foods you love or giving up satisfying, great-tasting meals.

Growing up in Southeast Asia, I experienced exotic foods, spices, and dishes from India, Asia, Spain, Hawaii, and Europe. Helping my mother in her culinary school from a young age taught me the skills of a trained chef. When I was nineteen years old my mother died and the culinary school became my responsibility. I managed to carve my own place in the food world—launching food trends, writing a weekly newspaper column, and opening restaurants.

My father was a physician who taught me a great deal about diet and health, so when I arrived in the United States over twenty years ago, I easily transitioned into the world of health care. Today, I own and operate several skilled nursing facilities in California.

But I have never lost my love of cooking. As I learned more about the effects of food on disease and aging, I was compelled to get back in the kitchen and create a cookbook that fused international and American flavors, familiar and exotic ingredients, and powerful nutrients that help the mind and body fight the diseases and wear and tear of aging.

The result was my first anti-aging cookbook—*The Age GRACEfully Cookbook: The Power of FoodTrients to Promote Health and Well-Being for a Joyful and Sustainable Life.* Based on the food-is-medicine principle, it features easy and flavorful recipes based on twenty-six nutrients in food that help prevent aging. I call these nutrients FoodTrients. You will learn more about FoodTrients on page 21.

Since the publication of *The Age GRACEfully Cookbook: The Power of FoodTrients to Promote Health and Well-Being for a Joyful and Sustainable Life,* I've continued to develop new flavorful and comforting recipes designed to keep you young, healthy, and beautiful. I've searched far and wide for better ways to incorporate the best nutrients into mouth-watering dishes that promote health and beauty—from the inside out.

Each recipe in this book is designed to deliver the nutrients you need for longevity with the flavor you demand. Each offers specific benefits for a lifetime of health and beauty. Each has been tested and retested by my FoodTrients team and has received a nutritionist's stamp of approval to ensure that you are benefitting from expert knowledge in the field of disease- and age-prevention.

For example, I promote using whole foods: ingredients that are unprocessed and unrefined to maximize their nutritional benefits, such as fresh fruits, vegetables, and spices; grass-fed beef, organic or free-range poultry, and fresh fish; low-fat or nonfat dairy products; dairy, butter, and sugar substitutes. Whole foods are available in supermarkets, health food and ethnic food stores, food co-ops, at farmer's markets, and through Internet searches. The chart on page 266 is an example of where I find some of the ingredients for my recipes. In many recipes, I provide alternatives for ingredients that are not as well known or may be hard to find.

In the pages that follow, you will find many easy recipes full of familiar FoodTrients favorites and a variety of new and exotic foods I've discovered in my continuing search for age-defying nutrients. It has been an exciting (and delicious!) journey for me, and I hope it brings you many satisfying taste adventures with dishes that you will want to eat over and over again.

Grace O

What Is a FoodTrient?

Wholesome foods have nutrients our bodies need to maintain optimum function. The recipes in this book are presented around an organizing principle I call FoodTrients®—twenty-six powerful nutrients that promote health, wellness, and longevity.

In time, a healthy lifestyle and a diet loaded with FoodTrients could add years to your life. You will get the most benefit from FoodTrients when they become the mainstay of your everyday diet, not from any one recipe.

FoodTrient Benefits

Since the publication of my first anti-aging cookbook, I've identified eight categories of FoodTrients that are essential to age-defying and healthful living. Specially designed logos represent each category and are indicated with every recipe along with summaries of the recipe's healthful properties. These benefits show how specific foods, herbs, and spices in the recipes help keep skin looking younger, prevent the diseases of aging, and increase energy and vitality. By incorporating these properties in your everyday diet, you are more likely to look and feel younger, have more energy, and improve your mood and mind. Who knew that the right foods in sufficient amounts could do so much good for your body? Now we have the science to prove it.

Ai Anti-Inflammatory: Reduces the inflammation process in cells, tissues, and blood vessels, helping to slow aging and lower the risk of long-term disease.

Ao Antioxidant: Prevents and repairs oxidative damage to cells caused by free radicals.

DP Disease Prevention: Reduces risk factors for common degenerative and age-related diseases (like cancer and diabetes).

IB Immunity Booster (including Anti-Bacterial): Supports the body's resistance to infection and strengthens immune vigilance and response.

M Mind: Improves mood, memory, and focus.

B Beauty: Promotes vibrant skin and hair and helps keep eyes healthy.

S Strength: Builds strength for bones, muscles and joints. Increases bone density, builds and repairs tissue.

WL Weight Loss: Encourages improved metabolism and digestion.

FoodTrients® at a Glance
The chart on pages 252–259 identifies the FoodTrients in my recipes, their sources, and their benefits to your health and well-being.

Getting Started

When it comes to great-tasting food and good health, I encourage everyone to be conscious of what they eat. I also urge cooks to use good-quality, organic ingredients whenever possible, but I understand that budgets and availability can make this challenging.

The recipes in this book deliver flavor *and* support longevity. How do I create them? I start with classic dishes, many of which I learned how to make from my mother, and I amp up their nutrient value with anti-aging superfoods, some of them exotic but easy to obtain. I research new ingredients constantly, always learning about antioxidant-rich foods from all over the world. I have a list of my favorite grains, vegetables, fruits, and legumes, proteins, and flavorings to use in my cooking (see pages 32–39), many of them derived from consultations with nutritionists.

Now that I have found how simple it is to incorporate FoodTrients® into my daily meals, it's time to share my method with you.

STEP 1 Avoid Saturated Fat, Refined Sugar, and Simple Carbohydrates

Taking time-tested recipes that I love—tapioca pudding, or prime rib roast, or chicken stew, for example—I first examine the recipe to make sure that it doesn't have too much saturated fat, refined sugar, or simple carbohydrates.

Saturated fat
If the classic recipe calls for chicken, I'll use skinless chicken. If it calls for chicken plus beef plus tofu, I'll pick just one of those proteins. I use lean beef or pork, and I make sure that I buy meat from farms that treat their animals well by not injecting them with hormones or feeding them too many antibiotics. I prefer grass-fed beef over corn-fed beef because cows were created to eat grass, not corn. The meat from animals that graze grass—cows, lambs, or even buffalo—contains more of the good-for-you Omega-3 fatty acids and less of the bad-for-you Omega-6s.

Refined sugar
Sugar, while safe in moderation, is a bitter enemy when it comes to aging, so I have looked for better substitutes wherever possible (see page 264 for healthy sugar substitutes). The reason I try to avoid refined sugar is because it causes inflammation—the enemy of anti-aging medicine. Also, many people have bad reactions

to white sugar and high-fructose corn syrup. Other sweeteners like honey, agave nectar, and coconut sugar contain vitamins and nutrients that are missing from white sugar. I've fallen in love with natural sweeteners like erythritol and xylitol. Xylitol has fewer calories than sugar but is very close in taste, and it kills bacteria in the mouth, which cause cavities and gingivitis. Erythritol, which has no calories, is cultivated through fermentation and is almost as sweet as table sugar. Stevia is one of the best natural sweeteners out there, but not everyone likes the taste, and it is not as easy to substitute in cakes and baked goods.

Simple carbohydrates

It is estimated that nearly a third of the population is sensitive to wheat. According to research by Mintel Business Net, 65 percent of those surveyed believe that eating gluten-free is healthier. Many of the recipes in this cookbook are gluten-free or offer gluten-free alternatives. Like many people, I have certain food allergies and food intolerances. Because I don't tolerate wheat gluten very well, I try to avoid refined white flour as much as possible. There are plenty of great-tasting alternative

grains to wheat that you can use, such as corn, brown rice, wild rice, quinoa, millet, flax, oats, amaranth, teff, and sorghum. Ancient grains that do contain gluten, such as emmer wheat, einkorn, spelt, farro, barley, rye, semolina, buckwheat, bulgur wheat, kamut, and triticale, are far more nutrient-dense than modern American high-yield wheat and so are better substitutes.

STEP 2 Add FoodTrients Favorites

Once I've stripped the bad stuff from my classic recipe, I add my FoodTrients Favorites: foods and spices that are rich in antioxidants and other anti-aging nutrients. I like to focus on vitamins, minerals, and other nutrients that specifically help to promote beautiful skin, lustrous hair, strong bones, free-flowing arteries, a healthy immune system, and a vibrant mind. I also gravitate toward foods that help fight cancer and other diseases. See my FoodTrients® Favorites (pages 32–39) and my Feel-Good Formula for Longevity, Beauty, and Wellness (pages 26–31).

STEP 3 Taste, Taste, Taste!

After I've added nutrient-dense anti-aging ingredients, it's time to test and re-test the recipe until it has the perfect balance of flavors, textures, and colors. I think it's important for food to look good, have an interesting texture— whether smooth or crunchy or a combination thereof—and be balanced in acidity and spice. I like to have a mix of recipes that, when served together in one meal, tingle all of the taste categories: sweet, sour, salty, bitter, and umami (an earthy flavor).

A FoodTrients recipe has to be so good that I want to eat it again and again. Otherwise, it can't be included in my cookbook. I'm a tough critic who's been cooking and creating world-renowned recipes for many years. Yes, food should make you look and feel younger with every bite. But it can't do that unless it tastes fabulous.

And that's my formula for creating delicious and healthy FoodTrients recipes for your daily health and beauty regimen.

Feel-Good Formula
for Longevity, Beauty, and Wellness

At FoodTrients.com, we're all about maximizing longevity, beauty, and wellness. And we know you are, too. With your health in mind, I've compiled a list of foods to eat in specific categories and for specific health benefits. Whether you want to eat for strong bones, beautiful skin, or a sharp brain, there's a roadmap for you.

ANTIOXIDANT (includes eyes)

To protect your eyes, skin, arteries, organs—and every cell in your body—from free radical damage, eat foods rich in antioxidants, especially vitamins A, C, and E, the mineral selenium, and the phytonutrients lutein and lycopene.

Almonds	Red grapes
Brazil nuts	Shellfish
Carrots	Strawberries
Citrus fruit (especially pink grapefruit)	Sunflower seeds
Kiwi	Sweet potato
Leafy greens (spinach, kale, collards)	Tomato paste, sauce, and juice
Red and orange peppers	Winter squash (butternut, acorn, pumpkin)

ANTI-INFLAMMATORY (includes allergies)

Anti-inflammatory nutrients can slow aging (especially of the skin), alleviate joint pain and allergy symptoms, and reduce risk of cancer, Alzheimer's disease, stroke, and heart attack. Anti-inflammatory nutrients include antioxidants (see the antioxidant-rich roods listed above), Omega-3 fatty acids, monounsaturated fats, as well as the FoodTrients curcumin, gingerol, oleuropein, and lauric acid.

Avocado	Garlic
Canola oil	Ginger
Fish and fish oils	Olives and olive oil
Flax, chia, and hemp seeds	Turmeric

BEAUTY

To protect against sun damage and skin aging, hydrate the skin, and reduce inflammation, steer toward foods containing antioxidants as well as Omega-3 fatty acids and monounsaturated fats.

Avocado

Carrots

Citrus fruit (especially pink grapefruit)

Fish and fish oils

Flax, chia, and hemp seeds

Leafy greens (spinach, kale, collards)

Olives and olive oil

Red and orange peppers

Strawberries

Sweet potato

Tomato paste, sauce, and juice

Winter squash (butternut, acorn, pumpkin)

BLOOD SUGAR MANAGEMENT

To stabilize blood sugar, avoid refined carbohydrates and sugar, exercise portion control, especially with fruits and grain-based foods, and include protein and healthy fats at every meal. Bitter melon and cinnamon have been shown to lower blood sugar.

Bitter melon

Chia seeds

Cinnamon

Fish

Flaxseeds

Legumes (peanuts, lentils, potatoes)

Lean meat

Nuts and nut butters

Poultry

Raw vegetables

Whole grains (in moderation)

BONES, JOINTS, AND MUSCLES

To increase bone density and reduce the risk of osteoporosis, eat foods containing vitamin D, calcium, magnesium, and soy isoflavones. To build and repair tissue, keep your protein up. Potassium and magnesium help prevent muscle fatigue and cramping.

Apricots
Bananas
Dairy
Edamame
Eggs
Fish
Meat
Miso

Nuts
Potatoes
Poultry
Seafood
Soy milk
Tofu
Whole grains (in moderation)

BRAIN AND MOOD

To aid circulation to the brain and reduce inflammation, eat foods containing allicin, anthocyanins, curcumin, Omega-3 fatty acids, resveratrol, and theaflavins. To buffer the effects of stress, eat foods containing B vitamins.

Berries
Brown rice
Coffee
Cranberries
Eggplant
Eggs
Flaxseeds
Garlic
Grapes
Kimchi
Kombucha

Nutritional yeast
Raisins
Red wine
Sauerkraut (unpasteurized)
Seafood (especially salmon and sardines)
Soy products
Tea (black and green)
Turmeric
Walnuts
Whole grains (in moderation)
Yogurt

CANCER PREVENTION

To lower the risk of cancer or inhibit tumor growth, eat foods containing anthocyanins, carotenoids, catechins, curcumin, fiber, indoles, isoflavones, isothiocyanates, lycopene, selenium, and sulfur compounds.

Brazil nuts

Broccoli

Cabbage

Cauliflower

Dark green leafy vegetables

Orange and yellow fruits and vegetables

Red, purple, and blue fruits and vegetables

Red wine

Soy products

Tea (black and green)

Tomatoes (especially tomato paste)

Turmeric

Watermelon

DIGESTIVE HEALTH

To promote good gut bacteria, help prevent constipation, and calm irritated bowels, eat foods containing fiber and probiotics. Fermented foods are especially good for the digestive system; buy unpasteurized versions because pasteurization can kill probiotic bacteria. Ginger contains gingerol, an anti-nausea compound. Mint has also been shown to calm the stomach. (See also Immune System, page 30, since the digestive tract houses most of our immunity-building cells.)

Chia, flax, and hemp seeds

Ginger

Kefir

Kimchi

Kombucha

Legumes (peanuts, lentils, beans)

Mint

Pickles (unpasteurized)

Pineapple

Sauerkraut (unpasteurized)

Yogurt

Whole grains (in moderation)

HEART (includes arteries)

Anti-inflammatory foods (listed above) can keep your heart and blood vessels healthy. In addition, foods high in vitamin K, folic acid, potassium, magnesium, allicin and resveratrol can help lower blood pressure, improve cholesterol balance, and keep the blood from becoming too sticky.

Almonds

Apricots

Bananas

Cranberries

Currants

Garlic

Green leafy vegetables (kale, chard, spinach)

Red grapes

Red wine

IMMUNE SYSTEM

To stimulate the immune system, eat foods containing vitamins A, C, and E, probiotics, selenium, and zinc.

Brazil nuts

Berries

Broccoli

Cheese

Citrus

Dark green vegetables

Kefir

Kimchi

Kombucha

Mushrooms

Onions

Orange and yellow fruits and vegetables

Sauerkraut (unpasteurized)

Shellfish

Yogurt

WEIGHT LOSS

To stimulate metabolism, help you feel full, and regulate your appetite, eat foods containing caffeine, protein, and fiber.

Apples
Chia, flax, and hemp seeds
Chocolate (dark)
Coffee
Eggs
Fish
Lean meat

Legumes
Lentils
Nuts
Poultry
Raw vegetables
Tea (black and green)
Whole grains (in moderation)

FoodTrients® Favorites

I've divided my FoodTrients Favorites into four categories: grains; fruits, vegetables, and legumes; proteins; flavorings (including spices and herbs):

Grains

Eating whole foods is essential for optimum nutrition and is a significant anti-aging strategy. Eating whole grains—and foods made from them—is part of this strategy. Whole grains have more nutrients than refined grains. Ancient grains—such as emmer wheat (farro), einkorn, Kamut (khorasan wheat), spelt, barley, rye, triticale, semolina, durum, and buckwheat—are far more nutrient dense than modern American high-yield wheat. They also contain far less gluten, so bread products made with these grains will be denser and chewier. That means they will fill you up, keep you satisfied for a longer period of time, and release their energy more evenly than refined white flour products will.

Each of these grains has its own merits, but as a group, whole grains contain three key FoodTrients: Omega-3 fatty acids for reducing inflammation, fiber for lowering cholesterol, and vitamin E for ensuring beautiful skin. They also contain vitamin B6 and tryptophan, a mood enhancer. And unlike simple carbohydrates, these whole grains contain D-chiro-inositol, which decreases blood sugar levels.

Emmer wheat, often referred to as farro—especially in Italy—is an older form of wheat similar to einkorn and kamut. These ancient wheats have a different number of chromosomes than modern wheat, making them more digestible and better for us. Farro has been found to stimulate the immune system. It also has a good amount of magnesium, which helps to lower blood pressure and build muscle. Einkorn contains the FoodTrient lutein, which helps promote eye health. Spelt is a modern wheat with forty-two chromosomes, but it's a heritage breed so it's not been genetically modified in any way. It has less gluten than high-yield wheat so it doesn't rise as high and can be substituted for all-purpose or whole-wheat flour in a one-to-one ratio.

Barley contains the FoodTrient selenium, which aids skin elasticity and reduces your risk of cancer. Barley and other grains can be malted or sprouted in order to make their nutrients more bioavailable. Rye and triticale—a wheat-rye blend—are high in antioxidants and grown in colder climates such as Scandinavia, Poland, and Russia. Buckwheat—used to make soba noodles—is rich in rutin, which can tighten up varicose veins. Semolina and durum wheat are ancient grains still in cultivation in Europe today. They are used to make pasta, so this is one carb that you don't have to avoid like the plague. Freekeh is wheat that is toasted while still green, which creates its unique flavor.

Here's one caveat: if you're allergic to the gluten in wheat (i.e., you have celiac disease or wheat allergies), eating whole-grain wheat is not healthy for you. Focus instead on gluten-free grains, such as corn, brown rice, wild rice, quinoa, millet, teff, oats, amaranth, and sorghum. Corn will raise your blood sugar faster than these other grains, so some nutritionists caution against eating too much of it. Brown rice has more vitamins and minerals than white rice and can be used in its place perfectly. I substitute brown rice for white in my recipes whenever possible.

Wild rice is really a grass so it's high in antioxidants, protein, and niacin. It also contains the FoodTrient zinc, which is critical to immune and thyroid function. Because of its tough texture, wild rice should be used sparingly or mixed with real grains such as brown jasmine rice.

Quinoa is a complete protein that contains all nine essential amino acids. Millet, another grass, is a classification of a few different small, round, seedlike grains. It's often used in birdseed in America, but in India they use it to make roti flatbread. Millet can be used in pilaf or couscous dishes or even popped like corn. Teff is made into injera flatbread in Ethiopia. It's a kind of millet with lots of iron and calcium. Oats are a delicious staple of American life that can help lower cholesterol. Tiny amaranth kernels are a pseudo-grain like quinoa and buckwheat, which means they are sources of complete protein. Sorghum is an African grain with powerful cholesterol-lowering properties. It's usually ground and used in gluten-free products.

I'm including seeds, such as flaxseeds, hemp, and chia seeds, in this category because they also have high amounts of Omega-3s and can sometimes work in recipes like grains. Flaxseeds must be ground or at least chewed very thoroughly in order to be digested. Hemp seeds are complete proteins that don't contain any mind-altering substances. Chia seeds, which help reduce blood-sugar levels, can be soaked in water to activate their gelatinous covering and then added to drinks. Other seeds, such as sunflower seeds, pepitas, and sesame seeds, can easily be added to whole-grain breads and bring more Omega-3s to the table.

Top 30 Grains

Top 30 Grains
Amaranth
Barley
Bran
Brown rice
Buckwheat
Bulgur wheat (cracked wheat)
Chia seeds
Corn
Durum wheat
Einkorn
Emmer wheat (farro)
Flaxseeds
Freekeh
Hemp seeds
Kamut (khorasan wheat)
Malted barley
Millet
Oats
Pepitas
Quinoa
Rye
Semolina wheat
Sesame seeds
Sorghum
Spelt
Sunflower seeds
Teff
Triticale
Wheat germ
Wild and red rice

Vegetables, Fruits, and Legumes

As anti-aging and other health experts know, the key to wellness is nutrient density and diversity—qualities that are found in colorful fruits and vegetables and legumes. Fruits and vegetables are loaded with antioxidants and disease-fighting nutrients. Legumes are full of fiber (one of my twenty-six FoodTrients) and B6 for energy. You literally can't eat enough of them (except for maybe white potatoes and corn, which have starches and natural sugars that aren't great for you in large quantities). The more fruits, vegetables, and legumes you pack into every meal, the more vitamins, minerals, and polyphenols—as well as the FoodTrients indoles, anthocyanins, and sulfur compounds, to name a few—you'll get. My FoodTrients Top 70 list focuses on the most nutrient-dense fruits, vegetables, and legumes from every corner of the world.

In *The Encyclopedia of Healing Foods,* Michael Murray describes vegetables this way: "Vegetables provide the broadest range of nutrients and phytochemicals, especially fiber and carotenes, of any class. They are rich sources of vitamins, minerals, carbohydrates, and protein, and the little fat they contain is in the form of essential fatty acids." *The Encyclopedia of Healing Foods* notes that fruits contain a form of sugar (fructose) that doesn't spike blood-sugar levels as quickly as table sugar (sucrose) or even white bread and similar refined carbohydrates. So if you're craving something sweet, grab a piece of fruit instead of a candy bar or pastry.

Most fruits and vegetables can be eaten raw, but some nutrients, such as the FootTrients lycopene and lutein (found in tomatoes and dark green leafy vegetables), are more bioavailable when cooked. Cruciferous vegetables, such as broccoli, cauliflower, and cabbage, are easier on the digestive tract and thyroid when cooked. Stir-frying, roasting, and steaming vegetables is preferable to boiling, because many vitamins are water-soluble and will be lost if you discard the water they have been boiled in. It can be beneficial to juice fruits and vegetables when they're fresh, but keep in mind that juicing removes most of the fiber.

Color is an excellent indicator of the nutrients found inside fruits and vegetables. Yellow and orange vegetables—such as squashes and pumpkins, citrus fruits, melons, papayas, jackfruit, mangoes, and camu camu—are a sure sign of the FoodTrient carotenoids. Carotenoids (beta-carotene and such) are crucial for making vitamin A. They inhibit certain cancers and tumor growth. They reduce the risk of heart disease. And together with vitamin C, another FoodTrient found in yellow and orange fruits and vegetables, carotenoids support immune function.

Red and blue fruits and vegetables—such as acai, berries, beets, eggplant, cherries, red chiles, figs, grapes, and plums—almost always contain the FoodTrient anthocyanins. Sometimes called anthocyanidins, this class of antioxidant inhibits the growth of cancer cells and improves capillary function, which is vital to a healthy brain. Some red vegetables and fruits—such as tomatoes, watermelons, guavas, and pink grapefruit—contain the FoodTrient lycopene. Lycopene lowers cancer risk, promotes prostate health, and aids cognitive function. Another FoodTrient, resveratrol—a heart-healthy anti-inflammatory—is found in red grape skins, cranberries, and currants.

Dark green leafy vegetables are in a class by themselves. That's because produce such as arugula, bok choy, broccoli, Brussels sprouts, collard greens, kale, mustard greens, rapini, and spinach all contain the FoodTrients isothio-cyanates, choline, and indoles. Isothiocyanates neutralize carcinogens to fight cancer. Choline (also found in soy, celery, and fava beans) prevents cholesterol accumulation, protects the liver, and balances acetylcholine levels in the brain. Indoles smell bad while cooking but detoxify the body and help prevent cancer. They are also found in every color of cabbage, cauliflower, onions, radishes, and garlic. Lutein, an eye-protective antioxidant, is another FoodTrient prevalent in dark green leafy vegetables.

The FoodTrient quercetin shows up in apple skins, pear skins, onions, and citrus. Quercetin supports the immune system, reduces inflam-mation, and may reduce allergic sensitivity. Legumes such as lentils, beans, peas, and peanuts, contain lots of the FoodTrients fiber and zinc, as well as B6, lysine, and D-chiro-inositol. Together these compounds reduce the risk of heart disease and cancer, lower blood cholesterol, boost energy, increase resistance to infection, and repair tissues like muscles and skin. It seems like there's nothing fruits, vegetables, and legumes can't do.

Top 70 Vegetables, Fruits, and Legumes

- Acai
- Apples (skin on)
- Artichokes
- Arugula
- Asparagus
- Avocado
- Banana
- Beets
- Bell peppers (red or orange)
- Bitter melon
- Black beans
- Blackberries
- Black-eyed peas
- Blueberries
- Bok choy
- Broccoli
- Brussels sprouts
- Cantaloupe
- Carrots
- Cauliflower
- Cherries
- Chickpeas
- Cranberries
- Cucumbers
- Currants
- Eggplant
- Elderberries
- Fava beans
- Figs
- Garbanzo beans
- Goji berries
- Grapefruit
- Grapes (red or purple) and raisins
- Green beans
- Green chiles
- Guava
- Jackfruit
- Kabocha squash
- Kale
- Kiwi
- Kumquats
- Lemons
- Lentils
- Limes
- Mandarin oranges
- Mangoes
- Mushrooms (especially wild mushrooms)
- Mustard greens
- Napa cabbage
- Oranges
- Papayas
- Pears (skin on)
- Peas
- Pineapple
- Plums (especially prunes)
- Pomegranates
- Pumpkin
- Rapini (sometimes called broccolini)
- Raspberries
- Red cabbage
- Red chile peppers
- Savoy cabbage
- Soybeans
- Spinach
- Strawberries
- Sweet potatoes and yams
- Swiss chard
- Tomatoes (especially tomato paste)
- White beans (cannellini)
- Zucchini

Proteins

Protein is very important for strong muscles and bones. Lean protein helps achieve weight loss. I love meat—it has riboflavin, vitamin B12, tyrosine, and the FoodTrient zinc—but I enjoy it in moderation, which helps protect against cardio-vascular disease. I also am careful about eating cured meats, which can aggravate joints and promote gout.

Whenever possible, I use grass-fed beef over corn-fed beef because cows were created to eat grass, not corn. The meat from animals that graze grass—cows, lambs, or even buffalo—contains more of the good-for-you Omega-3 fatty acids and less of the bad-for-you Omega-6s. And I make sure I buy meat from farms that treat their animals well by not injecting them with hormones or feeding them too many antibiotics.

Fish is known as a healthy source of protein. However, I avoid some fish, such as tuna, because the mercury content in older, larger, cold-water fish like tuna can be high. I also try to avoid eating any fish that isn't sustainable or is in danger of being overfished. Salmon and swordfish are good choices. Sardines have not only good fats, they also have lots of calcium. I love shellfish, although it can be high in cholesterol.

Eggs provide a form of protein that our bodies can absorb faster and easier than any other. They also contain the FoodTrient choline, an important brain chemical. Egg yolks have the FoodTrient lutein, which is great for beautiful, healthy, young eyes. Just like meat, eggs are great in moderation.

In addition to protein, dairy products provide calcium, phenylalanine (an important brain chemical), riboflavin, vitamin B12, and zinc. Yogurt has the added benefit of immune-boosting probiotics, which uncultured milk does not. Cheese also has probiotics, but some people can have adverse reactions to aged cheeses, while cream can add unnecessary calories and fat. Many people now drink fat-free dairy products, but they don't absorb calcium as well. Keeping all this in mind, I follow a dairy regimen of young cheeses, low-fat or evaporated milk, buttermilk (made by adding vinegar to milk), and yogurt.

Vegetable sources of protein abound. Soybeans and tofu are good selections, but those who have had breast cancer need to stay away from phytoestrogens like soybeans. Lentils, garbanzo beans, white beans, black beans, black-eyed peas,

Here are my Top 30 proteins for promoting beauty and longevity with every bite:

Top 30 Proteins

Almonds and almond milk
Black beans
Buttermilk
Brazil nuts
Cashews
Cottage cheese
Crab
Eggs
Fish (especially salmon, swordfish, tilapia, sardines)
Free-range chicken or turkey without the skin
Garbanzo beans
Grass-fed beef trimmed of exterior fat
Grass-fed buffalo
Grass-fed lamb
Lean pork
Lentils
Macadamia nuts
Moringa
Mozzarella cheese
Mushrooms
Ricotta cheese
Seitan
Shrimp
Soybeans
Spinach
Spirulina (algae)
Tofu
Walnuts
White beans
Yogurt (full fat or low-fat, but not fat-free)

and mung beans are all nutrient-rich protein sources. So are nuts, especially Brazil nuts—a FoodTrients favorite, with their high selenium content and walnuts, with their high amount of antioxidants. Mushrooms are a source of both protein and detoxifying agents. Another FoodTrient favorite, moringa, has incredible amounts of protein, even more than spinach. Seaweed and spirulina (a form of algae) are vegetable protein sources from the sea.

Flavorings

I like my food to be very flavorful. And I've learned that my spice chest can also be my medicine cabinet. So when I begin to create a recipe, I reach for the oils, herbs, spices, and sweeteners that will do my body good.

Fats are a very controversial subject. Butter, in particular, has gone in and out of favor with nutritionists over the last twenty years, but now the consensus is that butter, in moderation, is actually better for your arteries than margarine, trans fats, and hydrogenated fats or oils. Butter contains the FoodTrient zinc, which increases your resistance to infection; calcium and phosphorus, which help build and maintain strong bones, teeth, hair, and nails; B12 and riboflavin, which provide energy; vitamin D, which boosts the immune system; and the FoodTrient Vitamin E, an anti-inflammatory. I use butter in baking, but when I want to use a butter substitute in a recipe, I turn to Smart Balance buttery spread, which is a blend of butter and non-hydrogenated oils with Omega-3 fatty acids, another FoodTrient.

I've been telling everyone about the health benefits of coconut oil for years. Coconut oil is a medium-chain fatty acid, whereas animal fats are long-chain fatty acids. Although coconut oil is a saturated fat, your body can easily break it down because it comes from a plant. Studies have shown that coconut oil actually improves your cholesterol balance. It also promotes prostate health and is anti-microbial and anti-bacterial. An anti-inflammatory, coconut oil is good for your brain, arteries, and skin. You can even use it topically to reduce acne, fight fungus, heal wounds, strengthen hair, and keep skin hydrated and young-looking. I use coconut oil for sautéing vegetables—especially in Asian recipes. It's great for cooking rice in sweet or savory recipes and as a base for Indian curries.

I turn to olive oil when I want to make Mediterranean-flavored dishes. Olive oil has the FoodTrient oleocanthal and other polyphenols that work together as powerful antioxidants. It also contains Omega-3 fatty acids, which help reduce inflammation throughout the body as well as the risk of heart disease. Other vegetable oils, such as sesame seed oil, hemp seed oil, and flaxseed oil, are good sources of Omega-3 fatty acids and vitamin E.

Fresh aromatic vegetables, such as onions, garlic, and ginger, add more than just flavor to my recipes. They also help keep me young and healthy. I buy organic vegetables whenever possible. Onions contain quercetin, a FoodTrient that supports the immune system, reduces inflammation, and lowers allergic sensitivity. They also are packed with sulfur compounds and indoles, two FoodTrients that detoxify the body and help prevent cancer. In addition to indoles, garlic contains the FoodTrient allicin, which lowers cholesterol, reduces risk of a stroke because it thins the blood, and inhibits growth of bacteria. Ginger provides the FoodTrient gingerol, an antioxidant, anti-inflammatory

Top 35 Flavorings

- Agave syrup
- Allspice
- Basil
- Black pepper
- Black tea
- Brown sugar
- Butter
- Celery
- Chile peppers
- Cilantro
- Cinnamon
- Cloves
- Coconut milk
- Coconut oil
- Coconut sugar (or nectar)
- Dark chocolate
- Erythritol
- Flaxseed oil
- Garlic
- Ginger
- Green tea
- Hemp seed oil
- Honey
- Lemongrass
- Maple syrup
- Molasses
- Mustard
- Nutmeg
- Olive oil
- Onions
- Parsley
- Sesame seed oil
- Stevia
- Turmeric
- Xylitol

compound that alleviates nausea and decreases the risk of certain cancers.

Fresh herbs, when bright green and stirred into dishes raw (not cooked), contain the FoodTrient chlorophyll. I'm thinking of parsley, cilantro, and basil in particular. Chlorophyll can help purify your blood and manage bacterial growth. Lemongrass is a tasty, lemon-scented grass that contains citrol—an anti-fungal, anti-microbial antioxidant. Celery balances acetylcholine levels in the brain, keeping you in a good mood and your brain functioning optimally.

Spices are a veritable medicine cabinet. Everything from black pepper to allspice to cloves and cinnamon and nutmeg can enhance your health. Chile peppers are high in the FoodTrient vitamin C and in capsaicin, making them a pain blocker that protects your skin from sun damage and aging. Mustard contains indoles, and turmeric has the FoodTrient curcumin—an amazing anti-inflammatory.

I also like to cook with green tea and black tea because they contain the FoodTrient catechins as well as theaflavins and flavonoids that are all so good for me.

Sweeteners are a tricky category. I avoid high-fructose corn syrup like the plague because it's not a natural ingredient. Regular corn syrup has been jacked up into something our bodies don't handle well. It's best to avoid it altogether. White, refined table sugar has fewer nutrients than brown sugar or demerara sugar or molasses. Natural sweeteners such as honey, agave syrup, maple syrup, and coconut sugar or coconut nectar also have more nutrients than white table sugar plus some added health benefits.

All of these sweeteners will raise blood sugar levels, so if you have diabetes or need to keep your blood sugar low, use alternatives like stevia, a natural leaf, or xylitol, which has 9.6 calories per 4 grams (⅞ tsp.) and kills bacteria in the mouth, or erythritol, which has zero calories and is slightly less sweet than sugar. Dark chocolate isn't a sweetener per se, but it adds health benefits to sweet foods. Its catechins, flavonoids, and polyphenols help prevent cavities, shield against environmental toxins, help produce serotonin (a good-mood brain chemical), and may enhance weight loss.

part 2

RECIPES

appetizers

Crab-Mango Cocktail

When served in martini glasses, these crab cocktails make elegant appetizers for dinner parties. I use Alaskan king crab legs, but you can use grilled shrimp instead. Semi-ripe mangoes are more tart than fully ripe mangoes and hold their shape better. Depending on your taste for spicy food and drink, adjust the amount of hot sauce and jalapeños, or omit them. These cocktails are delicious alongside my Guacamole with Pomegranate Seeds (page 47) and tortilla chips.

1. In a glass bowl, combine the lime juice, scallions, jalapeños, salt, and hot sauce.

2. Fold in the mangoes, tomatoes, coconut meat, and cilantro.

3. Carefully fold in the crab meat without breaking it apart.

4. Chill in the refrigerator for at least 2 hours.

5. To serve, spoon into martini glasses.

Serves 4

½ cup fresh lime juice

¼ cup sliced scallions

2 tsp. sliced jalapeños

1–2 tsp. sea salt

1–2 tsp. hot sauce

2 cups diced green (semi-ripe) mangoes

1½ cups diced Roma tomatoes

1 cup julienned young coconut meat

¼ cup minced cilantro

1 cup steamed, coarsely chopped crab meat

BENEFITS Crab and other shellfish contain selenium, an antioxidant that increases resistance to infection. The mango, lime, and hot sauce deliver plenty of vitamin C, which helps the body resist infection and protects against skin aging.

Guacamole with Pomegranate Seeds

The idea for this combination comes from a very talented Mexican chef who owns an upscale restaurant in Santa Barbara. The pomegranate seeds add a spectacular, tart crunch to this otherwise mild dip. I serve this dip with blue corn chips, which add a splash of color and are higher in antioxidants than yellow chips.

1. Mash the avocado, lemon or lime juice, salt, and pepper.

2. Fold in the remaining ingredients. Serve with tortilla chips.

CHEF'S NOTE *Peel and seed the pomegranates under water so as not to stain your clothes or the countertop. The white pith will float while the seeds sink to the bottom.*

Yields 4 cups

3 cups diced avocado
(2 large avocados)

3 Tbs. fresh lemon or lime juice

Salt or salt substitute to taste

Freshly ground black pepper to taste

1 cup pomegranate seeds
(1 ripe pomegranate)

½ cup chopped cilantro leaves

¼ cup minced red onion

1 Tbs. minced jalapeño, seeded if desired

BENEFITS Avocados are full of monounsaturated fats, which help protect the skin from the aging effects of the sun. The anthocyanins in pomegranates have anti-inflammatory effects. Blue corn chips provide even more anthocyanins.

Olive and Watercress Tapenade

A heart-friendly snack, this tapenade is wonderful on crackers or warm bread and even dabbed on top of pizza.

Place all the ingredients in a food processor bowl and blend for 5–6 seconds. Scrape down the bowl and blend another 5 seconds or until the mixture is somewhat granular. Be careful not to overblend into a paste.

CHEF'S NOTE *Olives contain a lot of salt, so if you have hypertension or are watching your salt intake, avoid this recipe or use low-salt olives.*

Yields 2 cups

1½ cups tightly packed watercress, without stems

1½ cups tightly packed parsley, without stems

1 cup drained and pitted black olives

1 cup drained and pitted kalamata olives

1 cup drained and pitted green olives with pimentos

¼ cup olive oil

3 tsp. minced garlic

1 tsp. fresh oregano

BENEFITS Olives are full of monounsaturated fats, which are good for the heart. Garlic has allicin, another artery-friendly compound. Parsley is an excellent source of vitamin C (an anti-inflammatory), vitamin K, and folic acid, which also protect the heart.

Mangosteen Chutney

Mangosteens are a royal fruit, said to have been favored by Queen Victoria. They come from Southeast Asia, where I grew up. The hard, dark purple shell must be removed before you can get to the pure white, delicate, juicy segments inside. The largest segment of each mangosteen contains a pit that should be cut out and discarded. You can also substitute pears or peaches, or (to keep the dish exotic) rambutans. This chutney can be served with cheese and crackers, spread on burgers, or served alongside spicy Indian dishes.

1. Cook the onion, ginger, and garlic in the oil over medium heat for about 3 minutes or until the onions are translucent.

2. Add the sugar and continue cooking 1–2 minutes or until the mixture is sticky.

3. Deglaze the pan by adding the vinegar and scraping down the sides of the pan to remove any sticky bits.

4. Add the mangosteen pulp and seasonings. Reduce the heat to low and simmer for about 30 minutes, stirring often, or until the chutney is thick and bubbly.

Yields 3–4 cups

½ cup diced onion

2 Tbs. minced ginger

1 Tbs. sunflower oil

1 tsp. minced garlic

¼ cup raw or natural brown sugar

¼ cup apple cider vinegar

1½ cups mangosteen pulp (6–8 mangosteens)

¼ tsp. Chinese five-spice powder (optional)

¼ tsp. white pepper

1 bay leaf

BENEFITS Mangosteen juice has anti-inflammatory properties and the rind contains xanthones, which are antioxidant and anti-inflammatory. The rind isn't very tasty, however, so some people take it as a supplement. Quercetin in the onions supports the immune system and may reduce allergic sensitivity. Ginger is used to alleviate nausea and inflammatory conditions.

Melon Balls with Mint and Prosciutto

Melons are truly beauty-boosting fruits. They are incredibly good for your skin. Ricotta salata is ricotta cheese that has been salted and dried until crumbly. It's light and delicious and offsets the sweetness of the melons nicely. The prosciutto is a nice touch to this elegant appetizer, but is optional.

1. Make the mint syrup: In a small saucepan, combine 5 or 6 mint leaves, the sugar, and the water and simmer for 5 minutes. Remove the leaves and discard. Simmer the mixture another 5 minutes or until thick. Set aside until cool.

2. Place the melon balls on a platter and dress them with the syrup. Garnish with the prosciutto (if using), cheese, and remaining mint leaves.

CHEF'S NOTE *Another way to use the prosciutto is to cube and crisp it in a pan over low heat, stirring frequently, for about 15 minutes. Then sprinkle the crisps over the melon balls after drizzling them with the mint syrup.*

Serves 4

1½ cups cantaloupe melon balls or cubes

1½ cups honeydew melon balls or cubes

¼ lb. thinly sliced prosciutto (optional)

2 Tbs. crumbled ricotta salata (or Manchego cheese)

Mint syrup

10–12 whole mint leaves

¼ cup raw sugar

¼ cup water

BENEFITS Both cantaloupe and honeydew contain SOD (superoxide dismutase), a powerful antioxidant and anti-inflammatory that helps keep your skin young looking. Both melons have plenty of vitamin C, which boosts collagen production for beautiful skin. Cantaloupe also contains carotenoids, which contribute a healthy glow to your complexion.

AoDP

Vegetable Chips

Almost any vegetable or fruit can be turned into a tasty appetizer or snack using a dehydrator, but these healthful chips are delicious whether you make them in a dehydrator or in the oven. For this oil-free recipe, I combine kale, broccoli, and okra and add a dash of salt and cayenne pepper for flavoring. I like to blanch the vegetables first so that they retain their bright, beautiful colors, but it's not a critical step. Try using this recipe with sweet potatoes, apples, pears, or green beans. The possibilities are almost endless.

1. Cut the okra pods in half (lengthwise or crosswise), cut the broccoli florets into 1-inch pieces, and tear the kale leaves into 3-inch squares.

2. Blanch the okra and broccoli in boiling water with baking soda for 2 minutes. (The kale leaves don't need to be blanched.)

3. Drain the okra and broccoli and plunge them into the ice bath to set their color. Drain and dry on a cheesecloth or kitchen towels.

4. In a dehydrator, lay the vegetables on the racks with space between each chip. Dry at 130 degrees for at least 8 hours.

5. Season with salt and cayenne pepper to taste. Serve or store in a sealed container.

Yields 1–2 cups

1 lb. each okra pods, broccoli florets, and kale leaves

4 cups boiling water

¼ tsp. baking soda

2 cups cold water plus 2 cups ice for ice bath

Salt or salt substitute and cayenne pepper to taste

CHEF'S NOTE *Before drying, de-seed fruits and cut fruits and vegetables into small pieces or slices. To make in an oven, lay the vegetables or fruits on a parchment-lined baking sheet and bake at 180 degrees (or your oven's lowest setting) for 2–3 hours or until the chips are crispy.*

BENEFITS Kale and broccoli are green leafy vegetables that contain indoles and isothiocyanates (sulfur compounds), both of which demonstrate cancer-preventing properties. Kale, broccoli, and okra all contain lutein, which helps prevent macular degeneration. Okra also has vitamin C, which helps protect against heart disease and stroke.

appetizers 55

Annatto Hummus

Annatto seeds are a beautiful deep-orange color. I've amped up the nutrient content of this recipe by infusing oil with annatto. Serve the hummus with cut vegetables or spread it on pita wedges or flatbread.

1. Drain and rinse the garbanzo beans.
2. Place the beans, water, 1 Tbs. of the Annatto Oil, and the remaining ingredients into a food processor bowl.
3. Blend for about 10 seconds or until very smooth.
4. Scoop the hummus into a shallow bowl and drizzle with the remaining Annatto Oil.

Serves 2–4

15 oz. can chickpeas (garbanzo beans)

¼ cup water

2 Tbs. Annatto Oil (page 240), divided in half

1 Tbs. tahini

1 tsp. fresh lemon juice

½ tsp. crushed garlic

¼–½ tsp. sea salt

⅛ tsp. paprika

⅛ tsp. red pepper flakes

BENEFITS Chickpeas (garbanzo beans) contain fiber, which can lower cholesterol and keep appetite at bay. They're also a good source of folate, which helps protect against heart disease. Annatto is an excellent source of tocotrienols, a particularly potent form of vitamin E that helps lower cholesterol and protects the skin from the aging effects of the sun.

Spiced Nuts

Nuts are one of the healthiest snack foods in existence. They can and should be eaten any time of day. Dr. Oz eats a handful of nuts just before dinner to take the edge off his appetite. Nuts are also perfect for an afternoon pick-me-up with a cup of coffee or tea. You can use any variety of nuts in this recipe. Increase the amount of cayenne pepper for more heat or leave it out altogether and use chili powder instead for a milder taste.

1. Preheat the oven to 225 degrees.

2. Toss the nuts, sugar, and spices in a large bowl until thoroughly mixed.

3. Fold in the egg whites and mix until the nuts are well coated.

4. Spread the nuts on a parchment-lined baking sheet and bake at 225 degrees for about an hour, stirring every 20 minutes. The nuts will be crispy once cooled.

Yields 1⅓ cups

1 cup unsalted almonds

1 cup unsalted pecans

1 cup unsalted walnuts

⅓ cup coconut sugar or brown sugar

2 Tbs. FoodTrients® Dessert Spice Mix (page 248)

¼ tsp. chili powder or cayenne pepper

⅛ tsp. salt or salt substitute

⅛ tsp. black pepper

2 egg whites (organic, free-range, or Omega-3-enriched), beaten

BENEFITS Nuts contain fiber and healthy fats, which help reduce the risk of heart disease and aid with weight management. The catechins and flavonoids found in cocoa powder (used in the Dessert Spice Mix) are believed to reduce the risk of heart disease. Cocoa has even been shown to elevate mood. (No surprise there!)

Cashew and Avocado Dip

This creamy dip is delicious on crackers or raw vegetables. If you thin it out with more water, you can use it as a dressing for salads or steamed vegetables.

Place all the ingredients in a food processor bowl and puree for 1–2 minutes or until smooth.

Yields 2 cups

1 cup cashews (raw or roasted)

⅓ cup water

¼ cup avocado

3 Tbs. cilantro leaves

2 Tbs. fresh lime juice

1 tsp. salt or salt substitute

½ tsp. minced or grated ginger

¼ tsp. cayenne pepper

BENEFITS Cashews and avocados both contain anti-inflammatory monounsaturated fats, which help nourish and hydrate the skin and protect the heart and brain. Ginger is also a potent anti-inflammatory.

Stir-Fry Korean Glass Noodles

Korean glass noodles are made from sweet potato starch. Gluten-free and low-calorie, they have a springy texture and a neutral flavor. In Korean BBQ restaurants, this dish is known as Jap Chae or sometimes Chap Chae. In this recipe, I jazz them up with marinated meat, stir-fry vegetables, eggs, and a sesame sauce. By serving the noodles, meat, vegetables, and eggs separately, this becomes a perfect party dish: your guests can toss together exactly what they want. Traditionally these noodles are served with a scrambled egg on top, but you can omit it. You can use chicken or tofu instead of beef. This dish can also be served as a main course.

1. Make the noodles: Cook according to package directions and drain, place in a serving bowl, and sprinkle with the toasted sesame seeds. Boil the remaining noodle seasoning ingredients in a saucepan for 5 minutes. Pour over the noodles, toss, and set aside.

2. Make the meat: Combine the meat and its seasoning ingredients in a bowl and let sit for 10–15 minutes. Stir-fry in a wok or skillet over medium heat for 5–7 minutes or until well done. Set aside.

Continued on next page

Serves 4

Noodles

1 cup Korean sweet potato glass noodles

Noodle Seasonings

1 tsp. toasted sesame seeds

¼ cup low-sodium soy sauce or tamari sauce

¼ cup water

2 Tbs. raw or turbinado sugar

1 Tbs. sesame oil

Salt or salt substitute and freshly ground black pepper to taste

Meat

1 cup thinly sliced beef tenderloin

1 Tbs. raw or turbinado sugar

2 Tbs. low-sodium soy sauce or tamari sauce

¼ tsp. black pepper

1 Tbs. sesame oil

BENEFITS Sweet potatoes are full of carotenoids, antioxidants that produce vitamin A in your body. Vitamin A supports the immune system and keeps eyes healthy. Shiitake mushrooms contain selenium, an antioxidant mineral that also strengthens immune response. Mushrooms and beef both contain protein for building muscles.

Stir-Fry Korean Glass Noodles

Continued from previous page

Vegetables

¼ cup julienned white onion

2 Tbs. sesame oil

2 tsp. chopped garlic

1 tsp. peeled and chopped ginger

½ cup julienned shiitake mushrooms

½ cup julienned carrots

½ cup firmly packed whole baby spinach leaves, without stems

¼ cup julienned green onion

Salt or salt substitute and freshly ground black pepper to taste

Egg topping

1 tsp. olive oil

1 egg (organic, free-range, or Omega-3-enriched), beaten

Salt or salt substitute and freshly ground black pepper to taste

3. Make the vegetables: Stir-fry the white onions, garlic, and ginger in the oil over medium heat for 5 minutes. Add the shiitake mushrooms and cook another 1–2 minutes. Add the carrots and cook another 1–2 minutes or until the mushrooms are cooked through and the carrots are crisp-tender. Remove from the heat. Stir in the spinach leaves and green onions and allow them to wilt. Set aside in a bowl.

4. Make the topping: In a nonstick skillet, heat the olive oil over medium heat. Add the beaten egg and season with the salt and pepper. Cook through, omelet-style, for 2–3 minutes without folding or turning. Turn onto a cutting board and slice into strips. Set aside in a bowl.

5. To serve, combine all of the ingredients in a large serving dish.

soups

"Cream" of Broccoli Soup

This creamy soup is relatively low in fat and calories. Broccoli is so good for us, we should eat as much of it as possible. The baking soda preserves the green color of the vegetables.

1. Peel and cut the broccoli into 2-inch pieces and florets. Set aside about 8 florets.

2. Heat the butter in a large, heavy-bottomed soup pan. Add the potatoes and onion and cook over medium heat for 5 minutes.

3. Add the broccoli, water, bay leaves, and baking soda. Bring to a boil and then simmer for 20 minutes or until the broccoli and potatoes are tender.

4. Add the broccoli florets and cook another 10 minutes. Allow the soup to cool slightly. Remove the florets to use as garnishments.

5. Remove the bay leaves and add the yogurt.

6. Pour the soup into a blender (or blend by hand) and whirl for 3–5 minutes or until smooth.

7. Pour into soup bowls, add the reserved florets, and swirl with the extra yogurt.

Serves 4–6

1 lb. broccoli

¼ cup butter or Smart Balance

¾ cup diced potatoes

¾ cup diced onion

4 cups water

4 bay leaves

⅛ tsp. baking soda

1 cup plain low-fat yogurt, plus extra for garnish

CHEF'S NOTE *If you have one of those new cooking blenders by Cuisinart, this soup is even easier to make. Sauté the onions and potatoes right in the blender, add the water, broccoli, and baking soda, and cook. Then switch to blend mode. You might want to omit the bay leaves so you don't have to fish them out before blending.*

BENEFITS Broccoli has isothiocyanates and indoles, sulfur compounds with anticancer activities. The lutein in broccoli helps protect your eyes as you age. Broccoli also contains SOD (superoxide dismutase), a powerful antioxidant and anti-inflammatory that fights free radical damage to keep skin looking young. Calcium promotes healthy bones and helps regulate blood pressure.

Chicken Soup with Coconut Meat

I like to serve this soup in fresh, young Thai coconuts cut in half. This makes for a dramatic presentation and allows my guests to scoop up the young coconut meat as they eat the soup. I use my Homemade Chicken Stock, strain it, and pour it into the coconut shells along with the chicken meat. You can also use store-bought chicken broth instead of homemade. If young coconuts are hard to find, or if you don't want to cut them open yourself, you can always serve this soup in regular bowls and add young coconut meat.

1. Saw the coconut shells in half, reserving the coconut water, if possible, for another use. If need be, saw a bit off the bottoms of the coconuts so that they stand up straight on their own.

2. Add the shredded chicken meat to the coconut bowls.

3. Pour the hot chicken stock over the meat.

CHEF'S NOTE *If using coconut meat, cut into bite-sized strips and add ¼ cup per bowl. I buy packed raw coconut from Exotic Superfoods, www.exoticsuperfoods.com.*

Serves 8

4 young Thai coconuts

2 lb. shredded cooked chicken (white and/or dark)

1 recipe Homemade Chicken Stock (page 244)

BENEFITS Coconut has medium-chain fatty acids that are quickly metabolized and converted to energy and can also help quell your appetite. The lean protein in chicken provides the building blocks your body needs to build and maintain strong muscles and a robust immune response.

White Bean Soup

This hearty vegetarian soup makes a great meal or starter. I use my Homemade Vegetable Stock as a base, but you can also use store-bought vegetable broth. You can use white cannellini or navy beans instead of white kidney beans.

1. Drain the beans and divide them equally into 2 bowls. Mash the beans in 1 bowl. Keep the beans in other bowl whole. Set both bowls aside.

2. Heat the canola oil in a large stockpot with a heavy bottom. Cook the onion, tomatoes, and garlic over medium heat for 3 minutes or until the onions are translucent.

3. Add the vegetable stock, salt, pepper, and the mashed beans and bring to a boil.

4. Add the whole beans and the Swiss chard. Remove from the heat.

5. Ladle the soup into bowls and drizzle with the olive oil.

Serves 4

1 can (15 oz.) white kidney beans

1 Tbs. canola oil

¼ cup chopped onion

¼ cup chopped tomatoes

1 tsp. crushed garlic

3 cups Homemade Vegetable Stock (page 245)

2 tsp. sea salt

¼ tsp. black pepper

1 cup Swiss chard strips

2–3 Tbs. olive oil

BENEFITS Beans are loaded with protein and fiber, which makes them a great ally if you're trying to manage your weight. Fiber can also help regulate cholesterol and reduce your risk of certain cancers. Swiss chard has cancer-inhibiting carotenoids and vitamin C. Chard is an excellent source of vitamin K, which helps build strong bones.

Chicken Lentil Soup

Lentils are a good source of plant-based protein and fiber. Although the standard lentil soup contains plenty of protein, I like to add chicken and shrimp in a base of my Homemade Chicken Stock. You can also use store-bought chicken broth instead of homemade.

1. Soak the lentils overnight in enough cold water to cover.

2. Drain and simmer in 4 cups water for 30 minutes. Drain and set aside.

3. In a heavy-bottomed stockpot, heat the oil over low heat. Sauté the garlic and onion for 3 minutes.

4. Add the chicken and shrimp and cook for 5 minutes. Season with salt and a dash of ground black pepper.

5. Add the lentils, carrots, and celery, and cook for 5 minutes.

6. Add the chicken stock and eggplant. Bring to a boil over medium heat and then simmer for 10–15 minutes or until the chicken and vegetables are cooked.

7. Remove from the heat and add the spinach.

8. Add salt and pepper to taste.

Serves 4

1 cup dried lentils (or 2 cups precooked)

4 cups water

2 Tbs. coconut oil

1 Tbs. crushed garlic

¼ cup diced onion

1 cup diced chicken breast

½ cup chopped shrimp

Salt or salt substitute to taste

Freshly ground black pepper to taste

½ cup diced carrots

½ cup diced celery

4–5 cups Homemade Chicken Stock (page 244)

½ cup diced eggplant

2 cups whole baby spinach leaves, without stems

BENEFITS The fiber in lentils keeps you feeling full without added fat or calories. Fiber also helps escort cholesterol out of the body and reduces your risk of heart disease. Shrimp contains Omega-3s and selenium. Chicken is an excellent source of lean protein, which helps build up both your muscles and your immunity.

Minestrone-Style Soup

I make this colorful soup more nutrient-dense by using barley instead of noodles. Use whatever fresh vegetables you have on hand. You can also use store-bought vegetable broth instead of homemade.

1. Sauté the onion and garlic in the oil over medium heat for 3 minutes. Add all the remaining vegetables and sauté for 5–10 minutes. Season with the salt and pepper.

2. Add the vegetable stock and water (1–3 cups depending on desired thickness) and simmer for 30 minutes.

3. Add the barley and simmer another 30 minutes.

Serves 4–6

¼ cup chopped onion

1 tsp. minced garlic

1 Tbs. olive oil

1 can (28-oz.) crushed tomatoes (about 3 cups)

1½ cups chopped carrots

1½ cups chopped zucchini

1 cup corn kernels

1 cup chopped green beans

1 tsp. salt or salt substitute

¼ tsp. black pepper

3 cups Homemade Vegetable Stock (page 245)

1–3 cups water

¼ cup barley

BENEFITS Barley has vitamin E, which promotes beautiful skin; fiber, which controls appetite; beta glucans, which lower cholesterol; D-chiro inositol, which stabilizes blood sugar; and zinc, which boosts immunity. The lycopene in tomatoes lowers cancer risk and aids cognitive function. Tomatoes also contain anthocyanins, which inhibit the growth of cancer cells.

Seafood Chowder

Similar to French bouillabaisse, this broth-based soup contains saffron, white wine, and tomatoes. To make this recipe very easy, I start with a frozen seafood blend of shrimp, scallops, and calamari, and then add fresh clams, mussels, and cod. I like to leave the clams and mussels in their shells as long as the shells are thoroughly scrubbed.

1. In a heavy stockpot, melt the butter. Sauté the onion and garlic on medium heat for about 3 minutes. Add the tomatoes and celery and cook for another 2–3 minutes.

2. Add the water, potatoes, white wine, herbs, and seasonings and boil for 10 minutes.

3. Add the frozen seafood, return to a boil, and cook for 2 minutes.

4. Add the fresh seafood and boil another 3–5 minutes or until the seafood is opaque and the potatoes are tender.

CHEF'S NOTE *To make this dish with all fresh fish, use ⅓ lb. peeled and deveined raw shrimp, ⅓ lb. raw scallops, and ⅓ lb. raw calamari, or 1 lb. all shrimp. If you're combining fresh, frozen, and canned fish, add all the frozen seafood first, the fresh seafood next, and the canned seafood last. I use Trader Joe's seafood blend.*

Serves 4–6

1 Tbs. butter or Smart Balance

½ cup diced onion

1 Tbs. chopped garlic

1 cup diced Roma tomatoes

¼ cup diced celery

3 cups water

1 cup diced potatoes

¼ cup white wine

1 Tbs. fresh minced basil

2–3 tsp. salt or salt substitute

1 tsp. fresh minced thyme

1 tsp. fresh minced marjoram

¼ tsp. black pepper

¼ tsp. saffron

Dash of cayenne pepper (optional)

1 lb. frozen seafood mix (shrimp, calamari, scallops)

1 lb. each fresh clams, mussels, and diced cod (or salmon or tilapia)

BENEFITS The heart-healthy Omega-3 fatty acids in seafood can aid memory, lower dementia risk, and help fight skin aging. Shellfish contain selenium, an anti-inflammatory antioxidant that helps boost immune function and lowers cancer risk. Shellfish contains zinc for skin's collagen and elastin. It also helps reduce risk of macular degeneration and increases resistance to infection.

Orange Tomato Soup

My Homemade Vegetable Stock and Mock Sour Cream make this a light but satisfying vegan soup. You can also use store-bought vegetable broth instead of homemade. The bell peppers complement the taste and the nutrient content of the tomatoes. If you don't want to chop, seed, and peel the tomatoes, you can use canned chopped tomatoes instead of fresh.

1. Blanch the tomatoes in boiling water for 1–2 minutes, then drain and peel.

2. Chop the tomatoes coarsely and seed them.

3. Roast the bell peppers over an open flame for about 2 minutes per side or until the skin is blistered. Allow to cool in a paper bag for 5 minutes, then peel, seed, and coarsely chop.

4. Combine the tomatoes and peppers in a blender and blend until smooth.

5. In a stockpot, combine the tomatoes, peppers, and vegetable stock and bring to a boil.

6. Simmer for 10 minutes or until the soup is smooth and cooked through.

7. Add the salt and pepper to taste. Pour into bowls and garnish with Mock Sour Cream.

Serves 4

8–10 Roma tomatoes

2 orange bell peppers

2 cups Homemade Vegetable Stock (page 245)

Sea salt and black pepper to taste

¼ cup Mock Sour Cream (page 243), as garnish

BENEFITS Tomatoes have lots of lycopene, which lowers cancer risk and aids cognitive function. They also have anthocyanins, which inhibit the growth of cancer cells. Orange bell peppers have carotenoids, which have been shown to slow tumor growth. Bell peppers are also a good source of vitamin C, which reduces your risk of cancer and stroke.

Chilled Cucumber Soup

Chilled soups are so perfect on hot summer days. My Mock Sour Cream makes this cucumber-and-celery creation a vegan treat. This soup can be served as an appetizer, a main course, or even a palate cleanser between courses.

Serves 2–4

4 cups peeled, seeded, and chopped cucumber

1½ cups almond milk

1 cup chopped celery, strings removed

¼ cup Mock Sour Cream (page 243) (or low-fat sour cream), plus extra for garnish

2 Tbs. white balsamic vinegar

2 Tbs. parsley

1 Tbs. olive oil

½ tsp. minced garlic

½ tsp. salt or salt substitute

1. Combine all the ingredients in a blender and blend on high speed for 2–3 minutes or until smooth.

2. Chill in the refrigerator for 2–3 hours.

3. Serve in chilled bowls and garnish with Mock Sour Cream.

BENEFITS Cucumbers are a good source of vitamin K, an anti-inflammatory nutrient that benefits both your heart and your bones.

salads

Black Bean Salad

Black beans and pasilla chiles give this salad a Southwestern flavor and red wild rice makes it fun and different. A lime vinaigrette brings it all together. You can use regular wild rice and store-bought corn.

1. Toss the salad ingredients and chill in the refrigerator.

2. Whisk together the dressing ingredients.

3. Pour half of the dressing over the salad and toss thoroughly, evenly coating the rice, beans, and vegetables.

4. Chill for another 30 minutes.

5. Toss in the remaining dressing as desired and serve.

Serves 4

1 can (15 oz.) black beans, drained

½ cup cooked red wild rice

¼ cup julienned pasilla chiles (raw or roasted)

½ cup roasted corn kernels

½ cup julienned red bell pepper (raw or roasted)

½ cup diced, peeled, and seeded cucumber

½ cup chopped cilantro leaves

Dressing

⅓ cup white balsamic vinegar

2 Tbs. fresh lime juice

2 Tbs. olive oil

1 tsp. sea salt or salt substitute

BENEFITS Black beans and wild rice have protein for building muscles, bones, and blood, and fiber to aid with appetite control and weight loss. Red rice also contains anthocyanins, antioxidants that protect the heart. The red pepper adds lots of vitamins A and C, anti-oxidants that contribute to healthy, youthful-looking skin.

Asian Chicken Salad

In my version of Chinese chicken salad, I use mangoes instead of Mandarin oranges. The base of the dressing is a bottled sweet chili sauce. The crispy noodles, though not very healthy, are fun in moderation.

1. In a heavy skillet, fry the raw peanuts in the oil over medium heat for 5–7 minutes or until golden brown. Drain on paper towels and set aside.
2. Make the salad dressing: In a small bowl, mix the sweet chili sauce, lime juice, and oil.
3. In a large salad bowl, toss the cabbage, cilantro, and chives with half of the dressing.
4. Fold in the peanuts, chicken, and mango.
5. Garnish with the sesame seeds and crispy noodles (if using). Serve with the remaining dressing.

Serves 4

1 cup raw peanuts separated into halves

¼ cup olive oil

2 cups shredded Napa cabbage (white part only)

½ cup shredded red cabbage

½ cup minced cilantro leaves

⅓ cup minced chives

3 cups diced Roasted Chicken (page 129)

1 cup diced Mexican mango

2 Tbs. roasted sesame seeds

½ cup crispy chow mein noodles (optional)

Dressing
½ cup sweet chili sauce

2 Tbs. fresh lime juice

1–2 Tbs. sesame oil

BENEFITS Chicken is a great source of lean protein, which helps keep your appetite in check and maintain muscle mass. Cabbage contains indoles and isothiocyanates (sulfur compounds), both of which have anticancer potential. Vitamins C and A in mangoes fight inflammation and support immune function.

Ashitaba Potato Salad

Potato salad is a great way to showcase ashitaba leaves. These healthful leaves, grown in Japan and Southeast Asia, are often dried and ground for use as a dietary supplement. I grow my own ashitaba plants here in Southern California and I like to eat the leaves fresh. I like to use fingerling potatoes, but you can use small white new potatoes or Yukon gold potatoes instead, with a few blue potatoes for color. I prefer the French variety of green bean *(haricot vert)*, but American snap beans or pole beans will work as well. Apples give this salad a sweet dimension. I chose Fuji apples for their firm flesh, but almost any variety will do.

1. Cube or slice the potatoes and simmer in salted boiling water for 12–15 minutes or until tender but not mushy. Drain and cool.

2. Blanch the green beans in boiling water for 5–6 minutes and then shock them in an ice bath to set the color.

3. Combine the potatoes, green beans, apples, celery, and ashitaba leaves, and toss with the dressing.

4. Divide among 4 bowls and garnish with the ashitaba leaves.

CHEF'S NOTE *You can order an ashitaba plant from online sources or seeds for planting at Horizon Herbs, horizonherbs.com. I find this potato salad delicious even without the ashitaba leaves.*

Serves 4

1½ lb. fingerling potatoes

1 cup green beans, trimmed and cut into 1-inch pieces

½ cup cubed Fuji apple, skin on

¼ cup diced celery

½ cup young ashitaba leaves, torn into small pieces, plus extra, as garnish

1 cup Watercress Dressing (page 236)

BENEFITS The vitamin B12 in ashitaba leaves protects the heart and brain. Compounds unique to this species of plant, called chalcones, have antitumor, antibacterial, and wound-healing properties. The chlorophyll in ashitaba leaves and watercress helps deactivate carcinogens. Potatoes have plenty of potassium, which reduces the risk of osteoporosis and stroke.

Egg Salad with Turmeric

It's hard to beat the combination of eggs, celery, and turmeric for brain health. I use my homemade mayonnaise to make this simple, brain-building dish, but you can use store-bought mayonnaise instead. You can spread this egg salad on toast, eat it in a sandwich, or serve it on a bed of mixed greens. It's delicious with sliced tomatoes or thinly sliced scallions. For extra antioxidant power, add a few teaspoons of minced parsley or watercress. I prefer the taste of free-range hens (adult female chickens) whose yolks get their bright yellow color from the marigolds and grubs they graze on.

1. Place the eggs in a pan of cold water. Slowly bring the water to a boil over medium heat. Cover the pan, remove from the heat, and let the eggs sit for 7 minutes.

2. Drain the eggs and cool them in a bowl of ice water.

3. In a separate bowl, mix the mayonnaise, celery, relish (if using), capers, spices, and herbs.

4. Shell the eggs, then mash them with a fork or cut them into small cubes.

5. Fold the eggs into the seasoned mayonnaise.

CHEF'S NOTE *To make shelling the eggs easier, add a splash of vinegar to the cooking water. If you're serving this dish as a salad, refrigerate it first for a minimum of 2 hours.*

Serves 3–4

6 eggs (organic, free-range, or Omega-3-enriched)

½ cup Mom's Mayonnaise (page 235)

¼ cup diced celery

2–3 Tbs. pickle relish (optional)

2 Tbs. capers

1 tsp. turmeric powder

1 tsp. minced dill

1 tsp. minced chives

Salt or salt substitute and freshly ground black pepper to taste

BENEFITS Eggs contain choline, tryptophan, and phenylalanine, which contribute to healthy brain function and mood; zinc, which helps maintain collagen and elastin for beautiful skin; and the antioxidant lutein, which reduces the risk of age-related macular degeneration and cataracts. Curcumin in turmeric may ward off Alzheimer's disease, stroke, and even certain cancers.

Exotic Fruit Salad with Yogurt and Granola

Here's a protein-packed, vitamin-filled way to grab a healthy snack or start your morning. You can add spices, such as nutmeg, cardamom, and allspice (about ⅛ tsp. each), and nuts. Instead of exotic fruits you can use grapes, blackberries, strawberries, and/or bananas.

1. Preheat the oven to 325 degrees.

2. Make the granola: Toast the oats on a large rimmed baking sheet for 6–10 minutes, being careful not to let them burn. Reduce the oven temperature to 275 degrees. Warm the maple syrup in the microwave for 1 minute or until it is thin and runny. Toss with the oats, flaxseeds, sesame seeds, cinnamon, and salt.

3. Whisk the egg white and fold it into the granola mixture. Using a slotted spoon, transfer the granola to a parchment-lined or nonstick baking sheet. Leave any excess liquid behind. Bake at 275 degrees for 1 hour or until dry and crisp. Cool.

4. While the granola is baking, make the dressing: toss the lemon juice with the maple syrup and refrigerate for at least 1 hour.

5. To assemble, divide the yogurt among 4–6 bowls. Toss the fruit with the dressing and add the fruit salad to the bowls, evenly divided. Top with up to ½ cup granola per bowl.

Serves 4–6

2 cups oats

⅓ cup maple syrup

½ cup flaxseeds

¼ cup sesame seeds

1 tsp. cinnamon

Pinch of salt

1 egg white (organic, free-range, or Omega-3-enriched)

⅓ cup fresh lemon juice

2 Tbs. maple syrup

½ cup cubed fresh pineapple

½ cup longan, peeled, seeded and halved

½ cup sliced and seeded jujubes

½ cup sliced fresh jackfruit sections

½ cup peeled, sliced kiwi fruit

½ cup peeled, halved, and seeded rambutans

2 cups plain, low-fat Greek yogurt

BENEFITS The Omega-3 fatty acids in the flaxseeds are great for your arteries and heart. Oats and fiber are known to reduce cholesterol. The exotic fruits in this recipe are full of antioxidants and vitamin C, which help the body resist infection and aid tissue regeneration. The probiotics in yogurt can help digestion and bolster the immune system. Cinnamon can lower blood-sugar levels.

Shirataki Noodle Salad

Shirataki noodles are very popular. Made from yam fiber, these thin, white, gluten-free noodles are sold vacuum-packed. Because they have almost no flavor of their own, they must be served with sauce in order to be enjoyed. I created this salad with spinach and maitake mushrooms, also called hen-of-the-woods mushrooms because of their ruffled, henlike appearance.

1. Blanch the shirataki noodles in boiling water for 1 minute. Drain and pat dry.

2. Make the dressing: Combine the dressing ingredients in a jar, close the lid tightly, and shake well.

3. Cook the vegetables: In a sauté pan, warm 1 Tbs. of the oil over medium heat. Add the chopped garlic and ginger and cook for 1–2 minutes. Add the mushrooms and cook for 3–5 minutes. Add the spinach and cook for 1–2 minutes or until the spinach has fully wilted. Cool the vegetables in the refrigerator.

4. In a cold pan, toast the garlic in the remaining oil. Reduce the heat to low and allow to crisp slowly until lightly brown. Set aside to cool.

5. To assemble: Toss the noodles in a bowl with half the dressing. Add the vegetables and toss. Add the garnishes and toss. Serve with the remaining dressing on the side, if desired, or store it in the refrigerator for up to 2 weeks.

CHEF'S NOTE *If you use dried mushrooms instead of fresh, rehydrate them first in hot water for 20 minutes. You can use soba noodles in the same quantity as the shirataki noodles, but you will be adding calories and carbohydrates.*

Serves 2–4

7–8 oz. shirataki noodles

3 Tbs. sesame oil

1 Tbs. chopped garlic

1 tsp. peeled and chopped ginger

½ cup chopped maitake (or morel, chanterelle, or oyster) mushrooms

2 cups whole baby spinach leaves

4 cloves thinly sliced garlic

Garnishes

¼ cup julienned Persian cucumbers

1–2 tsp. toasted sesame seeds

1 Tbs. thinly sliced scallions

Dressing

½ cup seasoned rice vinegar

1 Tbs. sesame oil

1–2 Tbs. maple syrup or all-natural brown sugar

1 tsp. sea salt

Dash of white pepper

BENEFITS Shirataki noodles contain plenty of fiber without adding calories or carbohydrates. Spinach offers lutein for eye health. Ginger and garlic are natural anti-inflammatories. Maitake mushrooms have beta glucan, which may fight cancer cells and slow tumor growth. All mushrooms contain selenium, which lowers cancer risk and boosts immune response.

Arugula and Radicchio Salad

Arugula and radicchio are bitter lettuces that taste great with a sweet pomegranate molasses dressing. Pomegranate molasses is made by boiling down pomegranate juice into a syrup. A few ounces of goat cheese are excellent on this salad.

1. Make the dressing: Whisk the pomegranate molasses, oil, garlic, salt, and pepper until the molasses is well incorporated. Chill in the refrigerator for 1–2 hours.

2. Assemble the salad: Toss the arugula, radicchio, and fennel. Place in bowls and sprinkle with the walnuts and raisins. Serve with the dressing on the side.

CHEF'S NOTE *To make a pomegranate molasses with a less concentrated pomegranate flavor, mix ½ cup pomegranate juice with 3 Tbs. molasses.*

Serves 4

4 cups whole arugula leaves

1 cup shredded radicchio leaves

¼ cup shaved fennel

½ cup chopped walnuts

¼ cup golden raisins

Dressing

¼ cup pomegranate molasses

4 Tbs. olive oil

1 Tbs. crushed garlic

1–2 tsp. sea salt or salt substitute

¼ tsp. black pepper

BENEFITS Arugula has isothiocyanates and indoles, two powerful cancer-protective compounds. Radicchio contains lycopene, a cancer-fighting antioxidant, and lutein for eye and skin health. The anthocyanins in pomegranate inhibit the growth of cancer cells and improve capillary function for beautiful skin.

Shrimp and Grapefruit Salad

Pink grapefruit and shrimp come together nicely in this salad thanks to a rich, tangy buttermilk dressing. Though it is thick and creamy, buttermilk is actually low in fat. Whole romaine leaves give this salad a dramatic presentation, but you can chop them up. You can use white grapefruit, but you will lose some of the health benefits of pink grapefruit.

1. Peel and devein the shrimp. Toss with the oil and garlic.

2. Grill or boil the shrimp for 2–3 minutes per side or until it turns opaque. Remove from the grill or pan and allow to cool.

3. Make the salad dressing: In a food processor bowl, blend the dressing ingredients until smooth.

4. Toss the romaine lettuce in about 1 cup of the dressing. Divide among 4 plates.

5. Top the lettuce with the shrimp and grapefruit segments. Serve with the remaining dressing on the side.

Serves 4

1 lb. tiger shrimp

1 Tbs. grapeseed oil

½ tsp. crushed garlic

4 cups whole Romaine lettuce leaves

1½ cups pink grapefruit segments

Dressing

1 cup whipped low-fat or light cream cheese

¾ cup buttermilk

2 Tbs. flaxseed oil

⅓ cup sweet pickle relish, drained

¼ tsp. black pepper

¼ tsp. salt or salt substitute

BENEFITS Pink grapefruit is full of healthful compounds—anthocyanins, flavonoids, lycopene, polyphenols, quercetin, sulfur compounds, and vitamin C—that provide antioxidant power for promoting artery and heart health and protecting against sun damage and skin aging. Shrimp offer heart-healthy Omega-3s, plus selenium and zinc to help maintain a robust immune system.

Seaweed Salad

Seaweed salads are popular in Japanese restaurants. It's easy to make them at home. I like the wakame, dulse, and kombu or kelp varieties. The three varieties of fresh seaweed in this recipe (besides the nori) are the most common, but you can substitute arame or sea lettuce if you have it. If you are on a low-salt regimen, remember that seaweed can be high in sodium. I like to marinate and plate the seaweeds separately, but you can toss and marinate them together.

1. Soak the seaweed (not the dried nori) in lukewarm water for 15 minutes in separate bowls. Then rinse each seaweed (except the nori) in cold water 2–3 times.

2. Make the marinade: Combine the rice vinegar, oil, maple syrup or sugar, and seasonings.

3. In separate bowls, combine each type of seaweed with the marinade.

4. To assemble, lay the cucumber slices on 4 plates. Then add the salad mix and the tomatoes. Top with 3 separate piles of seaweed (one of each variety) and garnish with the nori.

Serves 4

½ cup fresh or salt-packed kelp (kombu) seaweed

½ cup fresh or salt-packed wakame seaweed

½ cup fresh or salt-packed dulse seaweed

½ cup Marukan seasoned rice vinegar

1 Tbs. sesame oil

1–2 Tbs. maple syrup or all-natural brown sugar

1 tsp. sea salt

Dash of white pepper

½ cup cucumber slices, skin on

2 cups spring salad mix

½ cup pear or grape tomatoes

¼ cup dried nori seaweed sheets, sliced or crumbled, as garnish

BENEFITS A great plant source of protein, seaweed also contains a lot of fiber, which can help control appetite, stabilize blood sugar, lower cholesterol. The alginate fiber in seaweed actually reduces fat absorption. Seaweed also has iodine, which helps the thyroid function properly, and chlorophyll, which binds to cancer-causing compounds and protects against certain cancers.

Couscous Salad

Couscous can be served warm or chilled. This North African grain is made from coarsely ground semolina (durum wheat endosperm) that is parboiled. It cooks up very quickly and can be tossed with any number of sauces and vegetables. You can use golden couscous, natural pearl couscous, or tricolor pearl couscous instead of the whole grain.

1. Make the dressing: In a large bowl, whisk together the oil and vinegar.

2. Pour half the dressing over the chilled couscous and toss thoroughly to coat the grains evenly.

3. Fold in the remaining ingredients and chill for another 30 minutes.

4. Toss with the remaining dressing, as desired, and serve.

Serves 4

2 cups cooked whole-grain couscous, chilled for 2 hours

½ cup cherry tomatoes, halved

½ cup roasted almonds

¼ cup minced chives

2–3 Tbs. whole, fresh mint leaves

¼ cup golden raisins

¼ cup radish slices

Dressing

2–3 Tbs. olive oil

¼ cup white balsamic vinegar

BENEFITS Whole-grain couscous has protein and iron for strength. Vegetables and couscous contain lots of fiber, which reduces your risk of heart disease and certain cancers. Almonds have protein and monounsaturated fats, which lower your risk of stroke and heart disease. The indoles (sulfur compounds) in the radishes help prevent cancer by neutralizing carcinogens.

Wild Rice and Quinoa Salad

This hearty, filling salad has a nice mix of textures thanks to the chewy grains, crunchy raw vegetables, and soft-cooked vegetables. The vinaigrette and dried golden berries add a sweet-sour tang. You can chill this salad for an hour or two to let the flavors blend, but I typically serve it right away.

1. In a bowl, combine the wild and brown rice in enough water to cover and soak for 1 hour.

2. Cook the quinoa according to package directions (they vary by brand) and cool.

3. In a large pan of salted water, boil the rices over high heat for about 25 minutes or until tender. Drain and rinse in a colander with cold water.

4. Make the dressing: Mix the dressing ingredients in a glass bowl.

5. Toss the cooked rice and quinoa with the dressing. Chill in the refrigerator.

6. Make the vegetables: Heat a sauté pan and add the olive oil. Cook the mushrooms and onions over medium heat for 5–10 minutes. Add the kale and cook for 1 minute or until wilted. Chill in the refrigerator for about 10 minutes or until cool.

7. To assemble: Combine the rice, vegetables, remaining raw vegetables, parsley, and golden berries and toss until the mixture is uniform. Add seasoning as desired.

CHEF'S NOTE *I rinse and soak the brown rice and wild rice before I cook them. Quinoa can be soaked, but it's not as crucial.*

Serves 4

½ cup each wild rice, brown rice, and red quinoa

2 Tbs. olive oil

½ cup diced cremini mushrooms

¼ cup diced onion

½ cup kale strips

¼ cup diced yellow bell pepper

¼ cup diced green bell pepper

¼ cup chopped celery

1 Tbs. chopped parsley

¼ cup dried golden berries

Salt or salt substitute and freshly ground black pepper to taste

Dressing

⅓ cup white balsamic vinegar

2–3 Tbs. honey or agave syrup

2 Tbs. low-sodium soy sauce

2 Tbs. flaxseed (or grapeseed) oil

1 tsp. sea salt

Dash of white pepper

BENEFITS Whole grains like brown rice, wild rice, and quinoa provide fiber, which keeps you feeling full to help you lose weight. Quinoa and wild rice are good sources of Omega-3s, which keep your skin looking fresh and youthful. Golden berries and red bell peppers contain both the immune-boosting vitamins A and C.

Curried Chicken Salad

Curry powder is so good for us that I eat it as much as possible. This salad gets an extra nutrition kick from Himalayan goji berries. I like to use leftovers from my Roasted Chicken (page 129) for this salad and serve it on a bed of lettuce. My Vegetable Crackers (page 232) are a perfect accompaniment.

Serves 2–4

1 lb. cooked organic or free-range chicken breast

½ cup roasted cashew pieces or halves

¼ cup raisins

¼ cup diced dried mangoes

¼ cup dried goji berries

¼ cup diced celery

Dressing

1 cup Mom's Mayonnaise (page 235) or your favorite brand

1 Tbs. maple syrup

1–2 tsp. curry powder

Salt or salt substitute and freshly ground black pepper to taste

1. Dice the chicken into 2-inch cubes and refrigerate in a large glass bowl.

2. Make the dressing: In a small glass bowl, gently whisk together the dressing ingredients. The dressing should be smooth and creamy with no lumps of curry powder.

3. Fold the dressing into the chicken cubes.

4. Fold in the remaining ingredients.

BENEFITS Turmeric, usually the main spice in curry powder, has curcumin—a powerful anti-inflammatory that helps prevent Alzheimer's disease. The anthocyanins in goji berries improve capillary function in the brain. Resveratrol in raisins also improves blood flow to the brain. Celery contains vitamin K, which helps keep heart and bones strong and healthy.

main courses

Vegetarian Stir-Fry Noodles with Annatto

These colorful noodles, which are made with my Annatto Oil and Annatto Water, are as delicious as they are healthful. They can be served as a main course, appetizer, or side dish. I use cornstarch noodles, but you can use glass or rice noodles. You can substitute other varieties of mushroom, and almost any cabbage will work—Napa, savoy, bok choy, green, or even red. You can use store-bought vegetable broth instead of homemade. This is a gluten-free dish, so I use tamari sauce instead of soy sauce. Bragg Liquid Aminos provides even more flavor.

1. In a large pan, sauté the onion and garlic in the Annatto Oil over medium heat for 3–5 minutes.

2. Add the mushrooms, Homemade Vegetable Stock, and Annatto Water and bring to a boil.

3. Add the cabbage, carrots, sauces, and spices and cover the pan. Reduce the heat to low and simmer for 10–15 minutes or until the carrots are tender.

4. Add the noodles and simmer another 3–5 minutes or until they are transparent.

5. Remove from the heat, toss thoroughly, and garnish with the lemon wedges.

CHEF'S NOTE *To make this dish heartier, add 1 cup of organic, free-range chicken breast strips to the pan when you add the mushrooms. If you use dried mushrooms instead of fresh, soak them first in hot water for 15–20 minutes or until soft.*

Serves 6–8

¼ cup Annatto Oil (page 240)

½ cup julienned white onion

1 tsp. minced garlic

1 cup julienned shiitake mushrooms

½ cup julienned wood ear mushrooms

4 cups Homemade Vegetable Stock (page 245)

¼ cup Annatto Water (page 240)

1 cup julienned cabbage

¼ cup julienned carrots

2 Tbs. low-sodium tamari sauce

1 Tbs. Bragg Liquid Aminos (optional)

Salt or salt substitute and freshly ground black pepper to taste

½ package (8 oz.) cornstarch noodles

Lemon wedges, as garnish

BENEFITS Annatto contains vitamin E for beautiful hair, skin, and nails. Shiitake and wood ear mushrooms are good sources of selenium, which lowers cancer risk and boosts immune function. Shiitakes also contain lentinan, which has anticancer properties. Cabbage is a cancer-fighter thanks to its indoles (sulfur compounds), which also make keratin in nails, hair, and skin.

Roasted Eggplant and Pepperoni Pizza

The small circumference of the Japanese eggplant yields perfect rounds for a pizza topping, but you can also use European eggplant. A few tablespoons of my Olive and Watercress Tapenade add zing, as do red pepper flakes. I add pepperoni for additional flavor, not for nutritional value. You can leave it out if you avoid eating cured meats.

1. Preheat the oven to 400 degrees.

2. Toss the eggplant slices in half of the oil (about 2 Tbs.) and the spices and lay in a single layer on a rimmed cookie sheet. Roast for about 40 minutes or until golden brown.

3. Brush the pizza crust with the remaining oil. Spread the crust evenly with the pizza sauce and sprinkle with the shredded cheese.

4. Arrange the pepperoni slices and enough slices of the eggplant to fill the pie. Dot with the Olive and Watercress Tapenade and bake at 425 degrees for 8–12 minutes or until the cheese is melted and lightly browned.

Serves 4

1 sliced Japanese eggplant (about 2 cups)

¼ cup olive oil, divided in half

¼ tsp. crushed garlic

¼ tsp. dried oregano

⅓ tsp. red pepper flakes

1 pizza crust or large flatbread

4 oz. pizza sauce

1 cup shredded, part-skim mozzarella cheese

16 slices pepperoni

3 Tbs. Olive and Watercress Tapenade (page 49)

BENEFITS The anthocyanins in eggplant improve capillary function for beautiful skin and a healthy brain. Olive oil contains heart-healthy monounsaturated fats. Garlic has allicin, which aids in cholesterol management. Lycopene in the tomato sauce is particularly good for prostate health.

Super Grilled Cheese Sandwiches

My Spelt-Oat Bread makes a healthier version of this classic American sandwich. You can also use a good rye bread. I use a light spray of olive oil instead of butter to brown the bread and add red peppers for their health benefits. Enjoy these sandwiches with a glass of dark red wine, such as Cabernet Sauvignon or Syrah.

1. Layer the bread with the cheese and roasted red peppers. Finish with the bread.

2. Lightly coat a nonstick pan or panini press with the oil spray and lay both sandwiches in the pan. If they don't fit, cook one at a time. Spray the top of each sandwich with the oil spray.

3. Cover and cook the sandwiches on medium-low heat for 5 minutes in the pan or until the bottom bread is golden brown. Carefully flip the sandwiches with a spatula, re-cover, and cook an additional 3–5 minutes or until the bottom bread has a golden crust and the cheese has melted through. If using a panini press, cook on low heat for 5–7 minutes.

Serves 2

4 thick slices Spelt-Oat Bread (page 237)

2 slices low-fat cheddar or soy cheese

6 roasted red peppers strips

Olive oil spray, as needed

BENEFITS Spelt contains choline and tryptophan, two brain-healthy compounds. The protein and calcium in cheese keep muscles and bones healthy. Red peppers are a good source of carotenoids, which protect your eyes, and vitamin C, which helps preserve youthful skin.

Vegan Mac and Cheese

I love macaroni and cheese, but I don't love eating all the animal fat in it. So I've created a vegan version. Quinoa pasta makes this comforting dish gluten-free, but you can use whole-wheat pasta instead. If the pasta isn't flavorful enough, try boiling it in my Homemade Vegetable Stock (page 245) or store-bought vegetable broth instead of water. You can use my Macadamia Cream (page 243) instead of the cashew cream and any variety of vegan cheese that you like. For a non-vegan version, try a low-salt, low-fat cheddar cheese.

1. Preheat oven to 350 degrees.

2. Make the cashew cream: Soak the cashews in the hot water for 1 hour. Drain and reserve half of the soaking water. Blend the cashews and the reserved soaking water in a blender for 4–5 minutes or until smooth.

3. Prepare the quinoa pasta according to package directions.

4. Drain the pasta, toss it with the oil, and spoon it into a 9 x 9-inch baking dish.

5. Mix the cashew cream and the vegan cheese (in a blender if the cheese is tough) and spread it over the pasta.

6. Top with the parsley, salt, and pepper.

7. Cover with aluminum foil and bake for 30 minutes.

CHEF'S NOTE *If you use roasted nuts, you may need to increase the soaking time to 2 hours.*

Serves 4–6

1 cup cashews (raw or roasted)

1 cup hot water

½ lb. quinoa pasta

2 Tbs. olive oil

1 cup vegan tree-nut cheese

¼ cup chopped parsley

Salt or salt substitute and freshly ground black pepper to taste

---

BENEFITS Nuts are chock-full of monounsaturated fats, vitamin E, and choline. Monounsaturated fats are anti-inflammatory and lower your risk of stroke, while vitamin E and choline support healthy brain function.

Quinoa Porridge

More and more people are eating the gluten-free grain quinoa because of its nutritional profile. This vegetarian entrée is modeled after a breakfast I had at a four-star resort while traveling abroad. Like oatmeal, it can be garnished with an endless variety of dried fruits and nuts. You can use plain or vanilla-flavored almond milk. For a more colorful presentation I use organic red quinoa.

1. In a covered saucepan, simmer the quinoa in the salted water for 15 minutes.

2. Add the almond milk and continue cooking for another 10–15 minutes or until the quinoa is very soft and most of the milk is absorbed.

3. Stir in the cinnamon and cool for 5 minutes.

4. Serve with the banana, walnuts, raisins, and maple syrup on the side.

5. Serve with more almond milk, if desired.

Yields 4 half-cup servings

1 cup red quinoa

2 cups water

¼ tsp. salt or salt substitute

2 cups almond milk

¼ tsp. cinnamon

1 sliced banana

¼ cup chopped walnuts

¼ cup raisins

4 Tbs. maple syrup

BENEFITS Quinoa is loaded with fiber, which helps you feel full and helps escort cholesterol out of the body. It also contains the brain-friendly nutrient choline, which many of us don't get enough of. Quinoa and walnuts have anti-inflammatory Omega-3 fatty acids, which regulate heart rhythm, aid circulation, and lower your risk of stroke and dementia.

Lemon Garlic Pasta

Lemon and garlic give this dish its zing. Roasted butternut squash and baby kale bring color and vitamins to the party.

1. Cook the pasta in boiling water according to package directions.

2. While the pasta is cooking, add 2–4 Tbs. of the oil in a sauté pan or skillet over medium heat. Add the garlic and sauté for 2 minutes. Add the squash and sauté until soft. Add the kale and lemon zest and season with the salt and pepper. Stir-fry on medium heat for about 5 minutes.

3. When the pasta is done, drain it and return it to the pot. Add 1 Tbs. of the oil and toss.

4. Add the vegetables, transfer the pasta to a serving plate, and spoon 1 Tbs. of the oil over the pasta.

5. Add the Parmesan cheese (if using) and garnish the serving plate with lemon wedges on the side.

Serves 2

½ lb. lemon garlic pasta (or regular spaghettini or capellini pasta)

4–6 Tbs. olive oil

4 Tbs. chopped garlic

1 cup diced butternut squash

1 cup baby kale

2 tsp. lemon zest

Salt or salt substitute and freshly ground black pepper to taste

Grated Parmesan cheese (optional)

Lemon wedges, as garnish

CHEF'S NOTE *Be sure to make the squash cubes small (about ½- inches square) so they can be scooped up with the pasta. If you use plain pasta, add 1 Tbs. fresh lemon juice to the recipe. I use baby kale because it's so tender, but if you use full-grown kale, cook it for about 5 minutes. You can find lemon garlic pasta at Pappardelle's Pasta, pappardellespasta.com*

BENEFITS The bright orange color of butternut squash signals the presence of carotenoids, which help fight cancer and also enhance the complexion. Kale also contains carotenoids plus vitamin A for boosting immunity, vitamin C for tissue regeneration, and lutein for eye health.

Chicken Curry with Moringa

Curries made with turmeric and coconut milk are amazingly heart healthy. Add some ginger and garlic and your heart and arteries will thank you even more. This dish will help reduce your risk of heart disease and stroke because of all of its anti-inflammatory compounds. If you can't find fresh moringa leaves, you can use green tea powder. To make this a vegan entree, substitute tofu or soybeans for the chicken. Vegan or not, this dish is delicious served over white or brown rice.

1. In a heavy, enamel-coated pot, sauté the onion, ginger, and garlic in the coconut oil for 3–4 minutes.

2. Add the chicken strips and cook another 5 minutes.

3. Add the curry powder and cook for 1 minute. Then add the fish sauce, salt, and pepper.

4. Add ½ cup of the coconut milk and bring to a boil.

5. Add the potatoes and carrots and boil for 15 minutes or until they are soft and cooked through, stirring frequently. Add ½ cup water if the curry is too thick.

6. Add the red peppers and remaining coconut milk. Boil for 5 minutes.

7. Remove from the heat and add the moringa and cayenne pepper (if using).

Serves 4

- ¼ cup onion strips
- 2 tsp. ginger strips
- 2 tsp. chopped or crushed garlic
- ¼ cup coconut oil
- ½ lb. chicken strips
- 2–3 tsp. yellow curry powder
- 2 tsp. fish sauce
- 1–2 tsp. sea salt
- ¼ tsp. white pepper
- 1 cup heavy coconut milk, divided in half
- 1½ cups diced potatoes
- 1 cup diced carrots
- ½ cup water, if needed
- ¼ cup red pepper strips
- 1 cup fresh moringa leaves
- ½ tsp. cayenne pepper (optional)

BENEFITS Curry powder contains curcumin, an anti-inflammatory as powerful as a prescription drug. The fiber in the vegetables helps lower blood cholesterol. Garlic has allicin, which thins the blood and also lowers cholesterol. Plant-based coconut milk contains the anti-inflammatory lauric acid. The potassium in moringa leaves helps balance sodium and regulate blood pressure.

Crock-Pot Chicken with Annatto

My fans love Crock-Pot cooking, so I developed this recipe just for them. The chicken is fall-apart tender after cooking slowly for hours. To add color, flavor, and vitamin E, I use some of my Annatto Water. I also add chorizo de Bilbao sausage to spice things up and plantains for a bit of sweetness. I serve this chicken with rice and fried plantains.

1. Rinse the chicken and pat it dry. Rub with the salt and pepper.

2. Place the chicken in the Crock-Pot and cook on medium heat for 4–6 hours or until the juices run clear and the bones pull apart easily.

3. Sauté cook the onion and garlic in the oil over medium heat for 3–5 minutes. Add the tomatoes and cook another 5 minutes.

4. Add the chorizo and Annatto Water and boil for 5 minutes.

5. Add the chorizo mixture, potatoes, garbanzo beans, and plantains to the Crock-Pot. Cook on the low setting for 30 minutes or until the potatoes are tender.

6. Add the cabbages and scallions and cook for another 5–10 minutes or until the cabbages are tender.

CHEF'S NOTE *If you don't have a Crock-Pot, you can use an enamel-covered, cast-iron pot in a 200-degree oven instead. You might need to reduce the initial cooking time, so check the chicken after 3 hours.*

Serves 4–6

1 (2–4 lb.) organic or free-range chicken (giblets removed)

1 Tbs. sea salt

½ tsp. black pepper

¼ cup olive oil

½ cup diced onion

1 Tbs. minced garlic

2 cups diced tomatoes

1 cup thinly sliced chorizo de Bilbao

½ cup Annatto Water (page 240)

2 cups quartered potatoes (about 4 medium-sized potatoes)

1 cup peeled garbanzo beans (cooked or canned)

4 plantains, peeled and halved

3 cups coarsely chopped Napa cabbage (about ½ head)

3 cups coarsely chopped green cabbage (about ½ head)

¼ cup julienned scallions

BENEFITS Annatto contains vitamin E, an antioxidant and anti-inflammatory that's great for your skin, hair, and nails. Chicken's lean protein preserves muscle tissue and supports immune function. The potassium in potatoes supports nerve and muscle function and promotes healthy blood pressure. Cabbage is a cancer-fighter thanks to its indoles.

Beer-Basted Chicken

This is my family's version of barbecued chicken. The brown sugar and the beer create a rich, dark coating for the chicken, which you start in the oven and finish on the grill. The beer also makes the chicken juicy and tender. We eat this dish with my Atchara Pickle (page 181) and Coconut-Lemongrass Rice (page 190). Serve it with a cold beer for added refreshment.

1. Cut the chicken into quarters and place in a roasting pan.

2. Combine the remaining ingredients in a bowl and mix well.

3. Pour the mixture over the chicken and marinate in the refrigerator overnight (or at least 6 hours).

4. Preheat the oven to 350 degrees.

5. Roast the chicken in the marinade at 350 degrees for 20 minutes or until halfway cooked.

6. Remove the chicken from the roasting pan and grill over medium heat. Pour any remaining marinade from the roasting pan into a bowl and use it to baste the chicken while it is grilling.

7. Grill, basting after 10 minutes, for 15–20 minutes or until the chicken's juices run clear when pierced with a fork.

Serves 4-6

1 (2–3 lb.) organic or free-range chicken

1 cup light beer

½ cup low-sodium soy sauce or tamari sauce

¼ cup fresh lemon or lime juice

⅓ cup honey or raw brown sugar

1 Tbs. Lea & Perrins Worcestershire sauce

¼ tsp. black pepper

2 tsp. sea salt

BENEFITS Chicken is chock-full of the heart-friendly antioxidant selenium. It also contains vitamin B12 to protect neurons and brain cells; lysine, which is needed for tissue repair; and copper for bone and joint health. The protein in chicken supplies amino acids that are needed to produce serotonin and dopamine for a calm, happy brain.

Chicken Meatloaf

My mother taught me how to make this meatloaf when I was a girl. The mixture will seem a bit loose in the mixing bowl, but it stiffens up just fine in the oven. I serve this dish hot with my Chicken Gravy (page 246) and mashed potatoes. I like to eat cold slices of the leftovers in a sandwich. To make this recipe gluten-free, use low-sodium tamari sauce in place of the soy sauce.

1. Preheat the oven to 350 degrees.

2. In a large mixing bowl, combine the chicken, Bragg Liquid Aminos, sauces, and chorizo until well blended.

3. In a separate bowl, beat the eggs with the salt and pepper. Mix in the remaining ingredients, except the oil spray.

4. Combine the egg and meat mixtures and blend well.

5. Line two loaf pans with parchment paper and spray with oil. Divide the loaf mixture evenly between the pans.

6. Bake at 350 degrees for 45 minutes or until cooked through.

7. Invert each loaf pan and remove the meatloaves. Carefully tear off the parchment paper.

CHEF'S NOTE *You can use ground turkey or pork instead of chicken.*

Serves 6–8

2 lb. ground organic or free-range chicken (all white or white and dark meat combined)

1½ tsp. Bragg Liquid Aminos

1½ tsp. Lea & Perrins Worcestershire sauce

1½ tsp. low-sodium soy sauce or tamari sauce

½ cup chopped chorizo (or 1 tsp. smoked paprika or pimento d'Espelette)

5 eggs (organic, free-range, or Omega-3-enriched)

1 tsp. sea salt

¼ tsp. white pepper

½ cup sliced roasted red bell peppers

½ cup sliced roasted green bell peppers (optional)

½ cup sweet pickle relish (or chopped pickles)

½ cup Parmesan cheese

4 Tbs. raisins, red (dark brown) or white (golden)

Olive oil spray, as needed

BENEFITS Chicken is chock-full of selenium, an antioxidant mineral that stimulates the immune system, and the amino acid tyrosine, a building block for dopamine, another brain-friendly chemical. Egg yolks contain brain-friendly choline, which prevents cholesterol accumulation; lutein, the cataract-fighting antioxidant; and vitamin D, which helps build strong bones, teeth, and nails.

Chicken Fajitas

Fajitas are a perfect party food because they can be assembled by your guests and the ingredients can be kept hot for an hour or two in a chafing dish. I use three different colors of bell pepper for eye appeal, but you can use only one. You can use other vegetables, such as mushrooms, scallions, zucchini, or even kale, cut long and thin. The cayenne pepper adds a little heat, which you can adjust to your preference.

1. Sauté the vegetables in the oil over medium heat for 5 minutes.

2. Add the chicken strips and seasonings. Cook for another 5–10 minutes or until the chicken is fully cooked.

3. Serve with the Flaxseed and Squash Tortillas, Mock Sour Cream, and Pico de Gallo.

Serves 2–4

1 cup julienned white onion

1 cup diced tomatoes

¼ cup julienned orange bell pepper

¼ cup julienned red bell pepper

¼ cup julienned yellow bell pepper

2 Tbs. olive oil

1 lb. organic or free-range chicken breast strips

1 tsp. sea salt

½ tsp. paprika

¼ tsp. white pepper

¼ tsp. cayenne pepper

1 recipe Flaxseed and Squash Tortillas (page 241)

1 recipe Mock Sour Cream (page 243)

1 recipe Pico de Gallo (page 233)

BENEFITS Chicken is an excellent source of lean protein. It also has detoxifying selenium as well as lysine, which repairs tissue. Bell peppers are loaded with vitamin C, which helps the body resist infection and aids tissue regeneration. Diets rich in vitamin C can reduce your risk of both cancer and stroke.

Roasted Chicken

I bought a turbo broiler because it cooks meats and fish so quickly. I was also attracted to the idea of eating freshly grilled foods without having to head outdoors.

Serves 4–6

1. Preheat the turbo broiler to 350 degrees.

2. Wash the chicken inside and out and pat it dry with paper towels. Place in a large pan and sprinkle with the salt and pepper.

3. In a small glass bowl, mix the sauces and the lemon juice to make the marinade. Baste the chicken with the marinade, inside and out, and marinate it in the refrigerator for 1 hour.

4. Remove the chicken from the marinade and stuff it with the lemons, onions, and herbs. Reserve the marinade.

5. Place the chicken inside the turbo broiler, directly on the rack.

6. Roast the chicken at 375 degrees for 10–15 minutes or until the skin turns crisp and brown.

7. Mix the oil and marinade and baste the chicken. Reduce the broiler temperature to 350 degrees and continue roasting for 30–35 minutes, basting again after 20 minutes. The chicken is done when the juices run clear and the leg bone easily twists away from the thigh bone.

8. Serve with the Chicken Gravy.

1 (2–3 lb.) organic or free-range chicken

2 tsp. sea salt

¼ tsp. white pepper

¼ cup low-sodium soy or tamari sauce

1 Tbs. Lea & Perrins Worcestershire sauce

1 Tbs. fresh lemon juice

1 lemon, cut into wedges

1 onion, sliced

3 whole bay leaves

3 Tbs. whole thyme leaves

3 Tbs. olive oil

1 recipe Chicken Gravy (page 246)

CHEF'S NOTE *To make this dish in a conventional oven, follow steps 1–4. Then, place the chicken in a roasting pan, cover with aluminum foil, and bake in a preheated oven at 350 degrees for 30–35 minutes. Baste, increase the oven temperature to 375 degrees, and roast for another 10–15 minutes or until the chicken is golden brown. The chicken is done when the juices run clear and the leg bone easily twists away from the thigh bone.*

BENEFITS Chicken has protein for building muscles and bones, vitamin B12 for healthy nerves and brain cells, and selenium, an antioxidant mineral that boosts immune function.

Mexican Chicken Lettuce Cups

I had a fork-and-knife salad similar to this dish while at a spa in Mexico. Of course, I put my FoodTrients spin on it to create this recipe. I serve it with my Guacamole with Pomegranate Seeds and Pico de Gallo, but it's also delicious with my Cashew and Avocado Dip (page 61). You can use steak strips instead of the chicken. You can sear the chicken fillets in a hot skillet instead of grilling them. Instead of the Pico de Gallo, you can use chopped Roma tomatoes and diced onions.

1. In a large Ziploc bag, combine the orange juice, oil, and spices and shake well.

2. Add the chicken fillets to the bag. Work the chicken and marinade with your hands for about 1 minute or until the chicken is well coated. Place the bag in the refrigerator and marinate the chicken for at least 1 hour.

3. Remove the chicken from the marinade and grill for 3–5 minutes on each side over medium heat or until the fillets are cooked all the way through.

4. To assemble, place 3–4 romaine leaves on each plate. On each leaf, spread 1–2 Tbs. of the guacamole. Then lay a chicken fillet, sprinkle with shredded lettuce, drizzle with the Pico de Gallo, and top with the cilantro leaves.

CHEF'S NOTE *If you're starting the recipe with whole chicken breasts, slice them into fillets no more than ¼-inch thick and a few inches wide.*

Serves 4

- ½ cup orange juice
- 1 Tbs. olive oil
- 1 tsp. sea salt
- ½ tsp. paprika
- ½ tsp. onion powder
- ½ tsp. crushed garlic
- ¼ tsp. white pepper
- ¼ tsp. chile powder
- ¼ tsp. ground cumin
- 1 lb. organic or free-range chicken breast fillets
- 8–10 whole romaine lettuce leaves
- 1 recipe Guacamole with Pomegranate Seeds (page 47)
- 2 cups shredded iceberg lettuce
- 1 recipe Pico de Gallo (page 233)
- ¼ cup whole cilantro leaves

BENEFITS Cilantro is full of antioxidants and disease-fighting phytonutrients. Chicken contains selenium, which protects cells from free radicals and lowers your risk of cancer. Selenium also increases resistance to infection. Avocados have oleic acid (also found in olive oil), which reduces your risk of heart disease.

Turkey Molé

You can make this dish in a slow cooker or on a stovetop. Traditional Mexican molé sauces can contain hundreds of ingredients, but I've kept this one simple. My FoodTrients® Dessert Spice Mix brings added antioxidants. For a spicier molé, add hotter chiles or more varieties of hot peppers. To make this dish gluten-free, spoon it into corn tortillas that have been warmed on the griddle or serve it over rice. You can substitute chicken for turkey, if you prefer, and use store-bought chicken broth instead of homemade.

1. Place all but the last 3 ingredients into an enamel-covered cast-iron pot with a lid. Cover and simmer for 30–45 minutes, stirring occasionally, or until the sauce becomes watery.

2. Add the dissolved cornstarch and cook another 5 minutes or until the sauce has thickened.

3. Remove from the heat and stir in the banana and chocolate chips. Let sit 2–3 minutes or until all the chocolate has melted. Stir well.

Serves 2–3

1¼ lb. skinless and boneless turkey cutlets or tenders

1 cup Homemade Chicken Stock (page 244)

1 cup almond milk

1 can (7 oz.) diced green chiles

¼ cup chopped jalapeño peppers, with seeds

2 tsp. hot sauce

1 Tbs. raisins

2 tsp. FoodTrients® Dessert Spice Mix (page 248)

2 tsp. raw or brown sugar

1 tsp. salt or salt substitute

1 Tbs. cornstarch dissolved in ¼ cup water

1 mashed banana

¼ cup dark chocolate chips

BENEFITS Turkey contains selenium, a potent antioxidant that also boosts immune function, and tryptophan, a precursor for mood-enhancing neurotransmitters. Dark chocolate provides tryptophan as well as heart-protecting catechins and flavonoids. The monounsaturated fats in almond milk are also good for the heart and circulation. Chile peppers are rich in vitamin C.

Squab Stuffed with Red Rice

I like to eat game meats like squab because they're sure to be free-range and organic.

1. Preheat the oven to 350 degrees.

2. Make the marinade: Mix the marinade ingredients in a Ziploc bag and place the squabs in the bag. Shake to coat well and marinate in the refrigerator for at least 1 hour.

3. Make the stuffing: In a sauté pan, heat 2 Tbs. of the oil over medium heat. Add the onion, cooking for about 3 minutes or until it is transparent in color. Add the turkey bacon and cook for 5 minutes. Add the rice, bay leaves, salt, and pepper, and cook for 5 minutes. Add the chicken stock and tomato paste. Stir well, reduce the heat to low, cover the pan, and simmer for 40–50 minutes or until the rice is almost done.

4. Remove the stuffing from the heat and add the red bell pepper. Allow the mixture to cool slightly.

5. Stuff the squabs with the rice mixture and place in a rectangular baking pan. Arrange any remaining stuffing around the squabs.

6. Cover with foil and bake at 350 degrees for 30–40 minutes.

7. Remove the pan from the oven and baste the squabs with the remaining olive oil. Return to the oven uncovered and bake the squabs for another 15–20 minutes or until they turn golden brown.

CHEF'S NOTE *If you don't have a local source for the squab, you can use two small Cornish hens or 1 large organic or free-range chicken instead. You can use store-bought chicken broth instead of homemade.*

Serves 2–4

2 fresh squabs, skin on

2 Tbs. olive oil

Marinade

4 Tbs. low-sodium soy sauce or tamari sauce

1 Tbs. fresh lemon juice

1 Tbs. Lea & Perrins Worcestershire sauce

1 tsp. sea salt

Dash of white pepper

Stuffing

4 Tbs. olive oil, divided in half

¼ cup diced white onion

½ cup diced turkey bacon

1 cup red or wild rice

4 whole bay leaves

2 tsp. sea salt

¼ tsp. white pepper

2½ cups Homemade Chicken Stock (page 244)

3 Tbs. tomato paste

¼ cup diced red bell pepper

BENEFITS Squab, Cornish hen, and chicken have protein and lysine for building muscle, bone, and blood, phosphorous for nerve and muscle function, and B12 for healthy brain and heart. Red rice boasts anthocyanins, the same phytochemicals that make grapes and olives so good for your heart.

Quail Adobo

This Philippine adobo is inspired by the original Spanish adobo. In the Philippines an adobo is meat cooked in a mixture of soy sauce, vinegar, and garlic. I like to top this quail adobo with onion rings that I've dehydrated and dried garlic slices, but roasted garlic is delicious, too. This recipe also works well with a large organic or free-range chicken.

1. Place the quail in a large, enamel-covered cast-iron pan with a fitted lid. Add the remaining ingredients except for 3 Tbs. of the oil and the water.

2. Bring to a boil over high heat. Leave the pan uncovered.

3. Add the water and cover the pan. Reduce the heat to low and simmer for 30 minutes or until the poultry is cooked through.

4. Once the poultry is cooked, remove the cover from the pan and simmer another 10–15 minutes or until the sauce is thick.

5. Remove from the heat and stir in the remaining oil.

6. Roast the garlic and onion rings in a 300-degree oven for 20 minutes. Garnish the quail with the garlic and onions (if using).

CHEF'S NOTE *If you use a whole chicken instead of quail, cut it into 8 serving pieces, double the ingredients, and eliminate the water.*

Serves 4

4 small quail

½ cup balsamic vinegar

6 Tbs. olive oil, divided in half

2 Tbs. low-sodium soy sauce or tamari sauce

1 Tbs. minced garlic

2 tsp. sea salt

¼ tsp. black pepper

½ cup water

Garnishes

¼ cup onion, sliced into rings (optional)

2 Tbs. garlic, sliced

BENEFITS The protein in quail and chicken helps maintain muscle mass and quell the appetite for a trimmer waistline. Olive oil contributes heart- and brain-healthy monounsaturated fats and polyphenols. Garlic is also a potent anti-inflammatory.

Wild Boar Kebabs

Wild boar has more flavor than tame pork. It has to be tenderized a bit, but that's easily accomplished with an onion-juice marinade. You can use pork or beef medallions instead of boar and any type of cubed vegetables. This recipe makes about 6 skewers.

1. Cut the medallions into 1-inch cubes.

2. Make the marinade: Mix all the marinade ingredients in a bowl.

3. Add the boar, cover, and marinate in the refrigerator for 1–2 hours.

4. Remove the meat from the marinade and alternately thread the meat and vegetables onto metal or wooden skewers.

5. Grill the skewers over medium heat, turning frequently, for 10–15 minutes or until the meat is cooked through.

CHEF'S NOTE *To make the onion juice, run two whole onions through a juicer to get the amount you need. If using wooden skewers, soak them in water for at least half an hour before threading.*

Serves 4

1 lb. wild boar medallions or pork tenderloin

½ cup each cubed white onion, red bell pepper, and green bell pepper

Marinade

⅓ cup xylitol (or coconut sugar or brown sugar)

½ cup low-sodium soy sauce or tamari sauce

¼ cup onion juice

3 Tbs. fresh lemon juice

1 Tbs. minced garlic

½ tsp. rock salt

¼ tsp. white pepper

BENEFITS Wild boar (and therefore pork) has protein and lysine for building muscle, bone, and blood. It also contains phosphorus for nerve and muscle function and vitamin B12 for protecting nerves and brain cells.

Buffalo Sliders

Ai Ao S

Buffalo (bison) are almost always raised on grass. Grass-fed meat (buffalo, steer, or lamb) is slightly higher in Omega-3 fatty acids, lower in Omega-6 fatty acids, and leaner overall. The flaxseed meal adds more Omega-3s. Dark red fruits like cranberries are a good complement to red meat. I grind them up so that the patties don't fall apart and mix them with flaxseed meal and breadcrumbs so that they don't form a sticky mass. Whole-wheat breadcrumbs also help low-fat meats stay tender while cooking over high heat. You can use any grass-fed meat or even ground turkey for this recipe. Because I watch my portion sizes, I prefer to make my patties small.

1. Pulse the cranberries, flaxseed meal, and breadcrumbs in a food processor bowl or blender for 1–2 minutes or until you have a coarse meal.

2. Combine with the meat, egg, salt, garlic, and vinegar. Shape into 8–10 patties, about 3 inches wide each.

3. Spray each patty with the olive oil spray and grill over medium heat (or broil under high heat) for at least 4 minutes. Flip the patties and cook another 4–5 minutes or until they are no longer pink in the middle.

4. While the meat is cooking, mix the goat-cheese spread ingredients and set aside.

5. Place the patties on the buns. Top with the cheese spread (or whole-grain mustard) and pickles (if using).

Yields 8–10 sliders

½ cup organic dried cranberries, sweetened or unsweetened

½ cup flaxseed meal

½ cup whole-wheat (or regular) breadcrumbs

1 lb. ground buffalo meat

1 egg (organic, free-range, or Omega-3-enriched)

1 tsp. salt or salt substitute

1 tsp. crushed garlic

2 tsp. red wine vinegar

Olive oil spray, as needed

8–10 whole-grain slider buns or rolls

Pickles, as garnish (optional)

Goat-cheese spread

¼ cup part-skim goat cheese

1 tsp. minced parsley

½ tsp. roasted garlic

½ tsp. fresh thyme

½ tsp. fresh dill

BENEFITS The protein in meat preserves muscle tissue as we age. Omega-3-enriched eggs bring additional anti-inflammatory benefits. Cranberries are full of antioxidants known as anthocyanins. Diets rich in these compounds have been associated with a lower risk of cancer and heart disease.

Ostrich Meatballs

In my family we call these meatballs albondigas. I tweaked this recipe by making the broth out of green tea and using ostrich meat from a local farm. You can use store-bought vegetable broth instead of homemade. You can use it instead of the green tea, but you won't get the same health benefits. You can use organic or free-range ground chicken or turkey instead of ostrich meat.

1. In a large mixing bowl, beat the egg lightly and add the salt, pepper, and soy or tamari sauce.
2. Fold in the ostrich meat and the flour until the mixture is smooth and even.
3. Fold in the white onions, parsley, green onions, and garlic and mix well.
4. With your hands, form the meat paste into about 12 medium-sized balls roughly 2–3 inches each in diameter. Place on a sheet of waxed or parchment paper.
5. In a large soup pot, bring the tea and Homemade Vegetable Stock to a boil.
6. Add the meatballs one by one while the liquid is boiling and cook for 10–15 minutes or until all the meatballs are floating on top of the liquid.
7. Add the diced vegetables and cook another 5–7 minutes or until they are crisp-tender.
8. Remove the meatballs from the heat and ladle them into bowls. Top with the cilantro.

Serves 4

- 1 medium egg (organic, free-range, or Omega-3-enriched)
- 1 tsp. rock salt
- ¼ tsp. white pepper
- 1 Tbs. low-sodium soy sauce or tamari sauce
- 1 lb. ground ostrich
- 1 Tbs. all-purpose or gluten-free flour
- ¼ cup finely chopped white onion
- 2 Tbs. minced parsley
- 1 Tbs. minced green onions or chives
- 2 tsp. minced garlic
- 2 cups brewed green tea
- 2 cups Homemade Vegetable Stock (page 245)
- ¼ cup each diced celery, carrots, onions, and tomatoes
- 4 Tbs. chiffonade of cilantro leaves

BENEFITS Green tea leaves are full of catechins, theaflavins, and safranal, which are all cancer killers. Ostrich meat contains copper, riboflavin, and selenium. Copper is a necessary component of collagen for healthy skin and joints. Selenium increases resistance to infection.

Chia Fettuccine with Southwestern Pork and Vegetables

Pasta infused with ground chia seeds is a bit chewier than traditional pasta but packs an extra nutritional punch. Pork, chiles, and Southwestern spices perfectly complement the taste and texture of this nutritionally dense fettuccine.

1. Mix the pork and the spices until evenly incorporated.

2. In a cast-iron or heavy-bottomed pan, cook the meat in 2 Tbs. of the oil over medium heat for about 5 minutes, stirring often.

3. Add the vegetables and remaining oil to the pan. Cook another 5 minutes.

4. Cook the pasta according to package directions. Toss with the meat and vegetables.

5. Garnish with the chopped scallions, Parmesan cheese (if using), and chia seeds.

CHEF'S NOTE *You can use 1 tsp. regular paprika or crushed red peppers in place of the piment d'Espelette; 1 can (4 oz.) green chiles instead of the pasilla chile; frozen corn instead of fresh; and regular or brown rice pasta instead of fettuccine. You can find BonaChia fettuccine at aldentepasta.com.*

Serves 4

1 lb. sliced pork loin

1 tsp. salt or salt substitute

1 tsp. minced garlic

¼ tsp. black pepper

½ tsp. dry mustard

½ tsp. ground cumin

¼ tsp. chili powder

1 tsp. piment d'Espelette

4 Tbs. olive oil, divided in half

½ cup chopped red onion

1 cup chopped red bell pepper

¼ cup sliced jalapeños

1 cup chopped pasilla chile

1½ cups fresh corn kernels

1 package (10 oz.) BonaChia Fettuccine

Garnishes

¼ cup chopped scallions

4 Tbs. Parmesan cheese (optional)

2–4 Tbs. black or white chia seeds

BENEFITS Chia seeds provide fiber, which helps with appetite control and blood-sugar stabilization, and can help regulate cholesterol. They also contain Omega-3 fatty acids, which are anti-inflammatory and lower your risk of stroke and dementia. Pasilla chiles and bell peppers have significant levels of vitamin C, which is good for helping the body resist infection.

Roasted Pork Shoulder

Pork shoulder is pretty tough, so I like to start this dish the night before and let it cook slowly overnight. This method will tenderize any tough cut of meat. The balsamic sauce can be made at the last minute. This is a perfect dish for a buffet dinner.

1. Preheat the oven to 200 degrees.

2. Rinse the pork, pat it dry with paper towels, place it in a large roasting pan, and prick it all over with a large fork.

3. Rub the pork with the salt. Allow the salt to penetrate the meat for 15–20 minutes.

4. Baste the meat with a little of the Annatto Water and put it in the oven.

5. Allow the pork to cook slowly for about 5–6 hours at 200 degrees, basting every hour if possible.

6. Make the balsamic sauce: Combine the sauce ingredients in a small bowl and mix well.

7. When the roast reaches an internal temperature of 170 degrees, remove it from the oven and allow it to rest for 20 minutes before carving. Serve with the sauce on the side.

CHEF'S NOTE *To make this dish ahead, prepare through step 5. Two hours before serving, roast in a preheated oven at 350 degrees for 1–2 hours, basting every half hour. Then resume with step 7.*

Serves 10–12

5 lb. pork shoulder

2 Tbs. rock salt or salt substitute

½ cup Annatto Water (page 240)

Balsamic sauce

¼ cup balsamic vinegar

2 Tbs. fresh lemon juice

1½ Tbs. low-sodium soy sauce or tamari sauce

1 Tbs. olive oil

½ Tbs. maple syrup

2 tsp. minced garlic (optional)

¼ tsp. rock salt

⅛ tsp. black pepper

BENEFITS Pork has protein and lysine for building muscle, bone, and blood, and phosphorus for nerve and muscle function. Annatto (achiote) seeds have a very bioavailable form of vitamin E, which helps lower cholesterol and protects the skin from the aging effects of ultraviolet radiation. They also contain carotenoids for healthy eyes.

Rack of Lamb with Fig Marinade

Figs can be dried and enjoyed all year long. I think they enhance the flavor of red meat, so I like to marinate my rack of lamb in a fig and onion paste. A fine red wine can also be used instead of the cooking wine and/or the pomegranate juice. Use the same wine you plan to serve at dinner for a nice pairing. A good Syrah or Cabernet Sauvignon would work well.

1. Soak the figs in the warm water for 1 hour. Combine them with the water and onion in a blender and blend for about 2 minutes or until a smooth paste forms.

2. In a saucepan, simmer the cooking wine over low heat for up to 15 minutes or until its volume has been reduced by half. Add the fig paste and stir thoroughly.

3. Remove from the heat and add the pomegranate juice, salt, and pepper. Stir again until well blended.

4. Place the lamb in a baking pan or Ziploc bag. Add the marinade, coating the meat entirely, and marinate in the refrigerator overnight or for at least 6 hours. If using a pan, cover it with plastic wrap.

5. Preheat the oven to 450 degrees.

6. Remove the lamb from the marinade and allow it to come to room temperature, about 20 minutes.

7. Transfer the marinade to a small bowl and whisk in the oil.

8. Sear the lamb over medium heat on the grill for 5 minutes on each side. Finish cooking it in the oven at 450 degrees for 7–15 minutes, basting often with the marinade. The internal temperature should read 145 degrees when done.

Serves 4

½ cup dried figs

½ cup warm water

½ cup coarsely chopped onion

1½ cups red cooking wine

2 Tbs. pomegranate juice

1 tsp. sea salt

⅛ tsp. black pepper

2 lb. rack of lamb

2 Tbs. olive oil

BENEFITS Lamb has protein for building muscle and plenty of vitamin B12, which protects neurons and brain cells. Figs contain calcium and potassium, which work together for proper nerve and muscle function. Calcium also helps keep bones and teeth strong.

Baby Back Ribs with Baobab Sauce

These ribs get their boost of flavor from a sauce made with baobab—an African fruit with a rather dry but antioxidant-rich pulp. I think baobab may be the next most exciting superfood. The dry, powdery fruit pulp has a tangy, lemon-like flavor that goes very well with barbecued ribs.

1. Preheat the oven to 350 degrees.

2. With your hands, pull off the underside of the ribs. Separate it from the meat and bones if necessary with a knife. Rinse the ribs and pat them dry with a paper towel.

3. In a small mixing bowl, combine the barbecue sauce, baobab powder, oil, garlic, and pepper. Mix well. You will use this mixture for marinating and basting.

4. Place the ribs in a glass baking dish. You may need to separate them into 2 or more slabs. Spread half of the baobob sauce onto the ribs and cover with foil.

5. Bake at 350 degrees for 1–1½ hours.

6. Transfer the ribs to a grill. Over high heat, sear the ribs for 4–5 minutes on each side, basting regularly with the remaining baobab barbecue sauce.

Serves 4–6

2 lb. pork baby back ribs

1 cup barbecue sauce

1 Tbs. baobab powder

2 Tbs. olive oil

1 Tbs. minced garlic

¼ tsp. black pepper

CHEF'S NOTE *In this recipe, you can use lemon juice or lemon zest (1 Tbs.) in place of the baobab powder, but it won't have the same health benefits. You can find Baobest baobab powder online at baobabfoods.myshopify.com.*

BENEFITS Baobab—though present in small amounts in this recipe—has antioxidants for aging gracefully, fiber for gut health, and vitamin C for reducing your risk of cancer and stroke. Ribs are full of protein for building muscle and bone. They also contain lysine, which is needed for tissue repair, plus phenylalanine and tyrosine, which build dopamine for brain health.

Beef on a Salt Block

Salt blocks from the Himalayas contain minerals that help balance the effects of sodium. This recipe calls for heating up large salt blocks in the oven and using them as a cooking surface. I sauce the beef slices after cooking with a dried fruit-Merlot reduction, but you can also use steak sauce. I like to set the heated salt block in the middle of my dining table on a trivet or other heat-resistant pad and let my guests cook their own meat. This recipe also works well with game meats, such as elk or venison. It's not recommended for those on salt-restricted diets.

1. Preheat the oven to 400 degrees.

2. Heat the salt block in the oven for about 1 hour.

3. Make the reduction sauce: simmer the wine with the dried fruit over low heat for 45 minutes or until thick.

4. Remove the salt block from the oven and set it on a heat-resistant counter or trivet.

5. Sear the beef on the salt block to your desired doneness: 20–30 seconds per side for rare, 1 minute per side for medium, or 2–3 minutes per side for well-done.

6. Remove the meat to plates and douse with the fruit-Merlot reduction.

Serves 6–8

2 lb. thinly sliced London broil or other tender cut of beef

Reduction sauce

2 cups Merlot or other red wine

½ cup dried cherries, cranberries, or raisins (or a combination)

CHEF'S NOTE *The longer the meat cooks, the more salt it absorbs. As the salt block cools, the cooking times become a bit longer. Don't let the meat sit on the block too long (no more than 10–15 minutes) or it will become too salty. You can find Himalayan salt blocks at kitchen stores and food shops.*

BENEFITS Beef contains vitamin B12, riboflavin, lysine, and tyrosine. Wine and cranberries have heart-protecting resveratrol. Cherries contain powerful antioxidants, cancer-preventive compounds, and anti-inflammatory properties. They also contain natural melatonin, which helps you sleep, and they can help relieve arthritis pain.

Salmon Poached in Pickling Spices

Pickle juice makes a nice poaching liquid, but I've found that pickling spices without the vinegar are even better for poaching fish, especially salmon. You can make your own spice mix or you can buy prepackaged pickling salts. I top this poached salmon with my Pecan and Sundried Tomato Tapenade and my Mock Sour Cream. It can be served hot or cold.

1. In a deep skillet, bring the water and pickling spices to a boil over medium heat.

2. Add the salmon, skin-side down, and poach for 20 minutes or until cooked through.

3. Spread a spoonful of Mock Sour Cream on each plate, lay a portion of the poached salmon on it, and top with a spoonful or two of Pecan and Sundried Tomato Tapenade.

CHEF'S NOTE *To make your own pickling spices, mix 3 tsp. dried dill, 1 tsp. salt or salt substitute, 1 tsp. mustard seeds, 1 tsp. fennel seeds, and ½ tsp. ground peppercorns. You can use smaller salmon fillets, but they will cook faster, so check them after 10 minutes.*

Serves 4

3 cups water

1 Tbs. pickling spices

2 lb. salmon fillets, skin on

1 recipe Mock Sour Cream (page 243)

1 recipe Pecan and Sundried Tomato Tapenade (page 231)

BENEFITS Salmon is an excellent source of heart-healthy Omega-3 fatty acids, which can also help improve cognition. Omega-3s beautify your skin by reducing inflammation and enhancing the skin's ability to retain moisture.

Asian Fusion Shrimp and Quinoa

Quinoa has become a popular ingredient, but it has almost no flavor. I've created a way of cooking this crunchy Incan grain that makes me crave it. You can use red, black, or white quinoa or a combination of colors. You can use chicken instead of shrimp and canned tomatoes instead of fresh.

1. In a medium saucepan with a lid, bring the water, salt, and lemongrass to a boil over high heat.

2. Add the quinoa, reduce the heat to low, cover, and simmer for about 15 minutes.

3. In a shallow pan, sauté the shrimp, vegetables, and garlic in the oil over medium heat for 3 minutes, stirring constantly.

4. Add the tomatoes, turmeric, salt, and pepper and cook an additional 3 minutes or until the shrimp are opaque and the vegetables are halfway between crisp and tender.

5. Remove the lemongrass from the quinoa.

6. To serve, spoon the sauce over the quinoa.

CHEF'S NOTE *If using chicken, cut a skinless, boneless breast (organic or free-range) into 1-inch cubes. Sauté the chicken and vegetables for 5 minutes (step 3).*

Serves 4

3–4 cups water

¼ tsp. pink Himalayan sea salt

1 medium-size stalk of lemongrass, cut into 3-inch pieces

1 cup quinoa

1 lb. peeled and deveined shrimp

¾ cup chopped orange or red bell pepper

¼ cup chopped scallions

1 tsp. crushed garlic

4 Tbs. coconut oil

1 cup crushed tomatoes

¼ tsp. turmeric powder

Salt or salt substitute and freshly ground black pepper to taste

BENEFITS Quinoa has plenty of fiber, which helps with weight loss. It's also an excellent source of folate, which protects the brain and heart. Shrimp contains Omega-3 fatty acids, which are heart-healthy and anti-inflammatory, as well as immune-boosting selenium.

Sardine Wrap

It's a snap to make this delectable sandwich. I like to make my own sardines and mayonnaise (see Mom's Mayonnaise, page 235), though canned sardines and store-bought mayonnaise work just as well. I add a few ashitaba plant leaves because they are so full of health benefits, but you can also use fresh parsley. I grow my own ashitaba plant because fresh leaves are hard to find.

1. Flake or mash the sardines with a fork. Remove the bones if desired.

2. Fold in the mayonnaise, celery, and onion.

3. Spread onto the flatbread and top with the carrots, jicama, and ashitaba leaves or parsley (if using).

4. Gently roll up the wrap and serve.

CHEF'S NOTE *You can order an ashitaba plant from a variety of online sources or seeds for planting at Horizon Herbs, horizonherbs.com.*

Serves 2

1 cup sardines

1 Tbs. mayonnaise

2 Tbs. chopped celery

1 Tbs. minced onion

2 large pieces of lavash flatbread

¼ cup shredded carrots

¼ cup shredded jicama

6–8 whole ashitaba leaves (or small bunch whole parsley leaves)

BENEFITS The Omega-3 fatty acids in sardines help reduce inflammation in the arteries, decrease the risk of stroke, ward off dementia, and keep skin hydrated and elastic. Sardines are also high in selenium, which keeps skin youthful. Chalcones—compounds unique to ashitaba—contain cancer-preventive properties and may also protect the skin from the sun's harmful effects.

Grilled Fish Tacos

These tacos are healthy and tasty. Even the garnishes and tortillas are good for you! I like Pacific cod fillets, but you can use tilapia or sea bass or any firm-fleshed white fish.

1. Marinate the fish in the lemon juice and salt for 30 minutes.

2. Brush the fish with the oil and grill or broil for 5–10 minutes on each side, depending on its thickness.

3. Blend the Mock Sour Cream with the cilantro for 1–2 minutes or until the mixture is pale green.

4. Place each fillet inside a Flaxseed and Squash Tortilla and top with the diced onion and shredded cabbage. Drizzle with the cilantro sour cream and dot with the Pico de Gallo.

Serves 3–4

1 lb. Pacific cod (rockfish) fillets

2 Tbs. fresh lemon juice

1–2 tsp. sea salt

2 Tbs. olive oil

1 cup Mock Sour Cream (page 243)

¼ cup whole cilantro leaves

1 recipe Flaxseed and Squash Tortillas (page 241)

½ cup diced white or red onion

1 cup shredded red or green cabbage

½ cup Pico de Gallo (page 233)

BENEFITS The Omega-3 fatty acids in fish are good for the heart, brain, and skin. The flaxseed tortillas contain fiber and Omega-3s, which can lower cholesterol and reduce your risk of heart disease. The indoles and isothiocyanates (sulfur compounds) in the red cabbage demonstrate cancer-preventive activity.

Flaxseed-Crusted Tuna

Flaxseeds and quinoa make a nice crunchy crust for tuna steaks. They also contribute substantial health benefits. You can use any firm-fleshed fish steaks in place of the tuna. You can use whole or ground flaxseeds and olive oil spray (as needed) instead of the oil.

1. Mix the quinoa and flaxseeds. Set aside.

2. Roll the tuna steaks in the salt and pepper and allow them to sit for at least 15 minutes.

3. Roll the steaks in the quinoa-flaxseed mixture.

4. Heat a cast-iron skillet over high heat for a few minutes. Remove from the heat, add the oil, and return to the stove.

5. When the pan is very hot, add the steaks and sear for about 5 minutes. Do not disturb the steaks until the crust has set.

6. Using a spatula, carefully turn over the steaks and sear on the other side for 5 minutes. Depending on the thickness of the steaks, the fish will be rare to medium at this point. Remove from the heat or continue cooking over lower heat to desired doneness, up to 5 minutes more on each side.

7. Remove the steaks from the skillet and drizzle them with the ponzu sauce.

Serves 4

¼ cup cooked quinoa, cooled

½ cup flaxseeds

4 tuna steaks (about ¼ lb. each)

1–2 tsp. sea salt

1–2 tsp. black pepper

2 tsp. olive oil

¼ cup ponzu sauce

BENEFITS Flaxseeds, fish, and quinoa all contain good amounts of Omega-3 oils, which are anti-inflammatory and lower your risk of stroke and dementia. Flaxseeds and quinoa have significant amounts of fiber, which helps escort cholesterol out of the body. Vitamin E, found in quinoa and flaxseeds, is another anti-inflammatory that supports healthy brain function and protects skin.

Salmon with Ginger-Apricot Sauce

You can make this nice anti-aging recipe year round. The salmon is poached, which keeps it moist. I favor wild-caught salmon from Alaska.

1. Preheat the oven to 350 degrees.

2. Place the salmon in a glass baking dish.

3. Combine the miso paste, water, 2 Tbs. of the ginger, 1 Tbs. of the garlic, and the oil and pour over the salmon.

4. Cover the salmon with aluminum foil and bake at 350 degrees for 30–35 minutes or until the fish is opaque. At this point it can be slightly undercooked because it will sit, covered, and finish cooking while you make the sauce.

5. Remove the poaching liquid from the baking dish, re-cover, and set the salmon in a warm place.

6. In a saucepan, simmer the poaching liquid and the remaining ginger and garlic over medium heat for 5 minutes.

7. Add the honey, apricots, salt, and pepper. Simmer another 10 minutes or until the sauce is thick.

8. To serve, top the salmon with the sauce and garnish with the green onions.

Serves 2

2 fillets fresh salmon (about 1 lb.), skin on or off

2 cups water

¼ cup miso paste

3 Tbs. minced or grated ginger

2 Tbs. crushed garlic

1 Tbs. peanut oil

1 Tbs. honey

½ cup chopped dried apricots, soaked in warm water for 1 hour and strained

Salt or salt substitute and freshly ground black pepper to taste

¼ cup sliced green onions, as garnish

BENEFITS Salmon has heart-healthy Omega-3 fatty acids, which can also help your brain function better and beautify your skin by reducing cellular inflammation that can lead to skin aging. Ginger and garlic add additional anti-inflammatory power. Apricots have carotenoids, which contain lots of antioxidant power and offer protection against cancer and heart disease.

Poached Cod à la Française

This simple recipe was inspired by a dish I had in France. It will work with any firm-fleshed white fish. The topping is nice on chicken as well.

Serves 4–6

4 fillets Pacific cod (rockfish) (about 2 lb. total)

Poaching liquid

½ cup water

¼ cup white cooking wine

1 Tbs. tarragon leaves

2 tsp. sea salt

1 tsp. lemon zest

Topping

½ cup sundried tomato strips

½ cup pimentos

¼ cup capers

4 Tbs. olive oil, divided in half

1. Make the poaching liquid: Put the poaching liquid ingredients into a large roasting or frying pan and cook on medium heat. The liquid should be about 1 inch deep. Bring to a boil.

2. Place the fillets in the liquid and simmer for 5–10 minutes or until they are cooked through.

3. Make the topping: Sauté the topping ingredients in 2 Tbs. of the olive oil. Cook for 3–5 minutes. Remove from the heat and stir in the remaining oil.

4. Drizzle the topping over the fish and serve.

BENEFITS Fish contains vitamin B12, which protects the heart and brain; selenium, which neutralizes free radicals; and Omega-3 fatty acids, which lower triglycerides and aid circulation. Olive oil contributes heart-healthy monounsaturated fats and disease-fighting polyphenols.

sides

Baby Bok Choy

Bok choy is best known as a supporting player in Chinese stir-fry dishes. Here I give it a starring role by boosting its flavor with tamari sauce and garlic. You can serve this with grilled chicken or fish.

1. Heat the oil over medium heat in a skillet. Add the garlic and sauté for 1 minute.

2. Add the tamari sauce and bok choy and sauté for 3–5 minutes, turning frequently, until the leaves are wilted and the stalks crisp-tender. The smaller heads will be done first. Remove them to a serving plate while the larger ones finish cooking.

3. Season with the salt and pepper.

CHEF'S NOTE *You can use full-size bok choy instead of baby bok choy. Just cut them in half lengthwise or increase the cooking time. You can also cook cabbage this way. Just cut it into long strips.*

Serves 2–4

2 Tbs. coconut oil or sesame oil

1 Tbs. minced garlic

1 Tbs. low-sodium tamari sauce

6 cups baby bok choy (4–5 heads)

Salt or salt substitute and freshly ground black pepper to taste

BENEFITS Bok choy is part of the cabbage family so it's loaded with indoles (sulfur compounds), which help to prevent cancer by neutralizing carcinogens. These compounds are also needed to make keratin for healthy nails, hair, and skin.

Garlicky Green Beans

These green beans are easy to make. They can even be prepped a day ahead of time, so they are perfect for holidays and dinner parties. Marcona almonds make this simple side dish elegant.

1. Blanch the green beans in a large pot of boiling water for 3 minutes. Drain and plunge into an ice bath to set the color. Pat dry with a paper towel.

2. Heat the oil in a pan over medium heat, add the green beans, and sauté for 3–5 minutes or until crisp-tender.

3. Remove the beans from the heat and toss with the remaining ingredients.

CHEF'S NOTE *You can start this recipe a day or so ahead of time: After blanching the beans, wrap them in a paper towel to retain moisture and refrigerate until you are ready to complete the recipe.*

Serves 4–6

6 cups green beans (about 1 lb.), trimmed

2 Tbs. olive oil

2 Tbs. Marcona almonds

2 Tbs. lemon juice

1 Tbs. chopped fresh parsley

1 Tbs. chopped fresh rosemary

2 tsp. minced garlic

½ tsp. salt or salt substitute

BENEFITS Green beans contain vitamins A and C. Vitamin A is an antioxidant that boosts immune function and keeps eyes and skin healthy. Vitamin C helps the body resist infection, prevent cataracts, and boost collagen.

Celery Root Mashed Potatoes

Celery root (celeriac or knob celery) gets no respect. Sure, it's somewhat ugly, but so are other tubers that grow underground. This mild vegetable is low in carbohydrates, full of fiber, and can pair well with higher-carb vegetables like potatoes. In fact, your guests might not even notice that these mashed potatoes taste any different.

1. Boil the celery root in a large pot of water for 20–30 minutes or until soft.

2. Boil the potatoes in another large pot of water for 15–20 minutes or until soft.

3. Drain and mash the celery root.

4. Drain the potatoes and mash them into the celery root.

5. Fold in the buttermilk and remaining ingredients.

Serves 4–6

2 cups cubed celery root, peeled

2 cups cubed Yukon Gold potatoes

½–1 cup buttermilk (depending on desired consistency)

1 Tbs. fresh chopped chives

1 Tbs. fresh chopped parsley

½ tsp. salt or salt substitute

½ tsp. crushed garlic

BENEFITS Celery root is rich in vitamin K, which helps your blood clot normally (good for your heart, circulation system, and brain). It also has phosphorus, which helps nerves and muscles function properly and strengthens teeth. Potatoes are a surprisingly good source of the skin-protective antioxidant vitamin C.

Swiss Chard and Kale Combo

It's hard to find a vegetable that does more for your longevity than kale. In this dish it's paired with mild Swiss chard and sweetened with apple cider and dried fruit. This combo is wonderful alongside chicken, turkey, or pork. You can use any variety of kale and grape juice instead of apple cider. A combination of the dried fruits makes a colorful presentation.

1. Heat the oil over medium heat in a skillet.

2. Add the kale, chard, garlic, and salt and sauté for 2–3 minutes, stirring frequently.

3. Add the cider. Cover the pan, reduce the heat, and simmer for 5–10 minutes or until most of the cider is absorbed.

4. Remove from the heat and toss in the dried fruit.

CHEF'S NOTE *Just about any dark green leafy vegetable can be cooked this way. If you use softer greens like baby kale or spinach, just decrease the cooking time slightly in steps 2 and 3.*

Serves 2–4

2 Tbs. olive oil

2 cups chopped kale

2 cups chopped Swiss chard

¼ tsp. minced garlic

⅛ tsp. salt or salt substitute

½ cup apple cider

¼ cup dried cranberries, raisins, or cherries

BENEFITS Kale contains indoles (sulfur compounds), which help to prevent cancer by neutralizing carcinogens. Kale and Swiss chard both have carotenoids and vitamin C—two great immune-system supporters.

Weller Red Cabbage

My friend Barbara Weller and her husband, Robb, love to cook. This is the Weller family recipe for red cabbage with bacon. You can leave out the bacon if you're not feeling decadent. This dish goes very well with turkey and game meats like venison or buffalo.

1. Broil the bacon in the oven for 5–7 minutes or until it begins sizzling on top. Turn over and broil another 3–5 minutes or until crisp.

2. Drain the bacon, cool on paper towels, and crumble into small pieces. Place in a small serving dish and set aside.

3. In a heavy enamel-covered or glass pan over medium heat, warm the oil and melt the butter.

4. Add the onion and sauté about 5 minutes or until translucent.

5. Add the cabbage, vinegar, and water. Reduce the heat and cook, covered, for 30 minutes, stirring occasionally.

6. Uncover, stir in the xylitol or sugar, and cook an additional 3–5 minutes or until the xylitol or sugar has fully dissolved and the cabbage is tender.

7. Serve with the crumbled bacon on the side.

Serves 2–4

2 slices uncured bacon

1 Tbs. olive oil

½ Tbs. butter

¾ cup sliced onion (red, brown, or white)

2 cups shredded red cabbage

½ cup apple cider vinegar

2 Tbs. water

½ cup xylitol or brown sugar

BENEFITS Cabbage contains indoles (sulfur compounds) and anthocyanins, a one-two punch for protection against cancer. Anthocyanins also help improve capillary function for better blood flow to the brain, eyes, and skin.

Tropical Yams

Heart-friendly yams are tarted up with lime juice and shredded coconut in this festive side dish. Serve it with lamb or my Ostrich Meatballs (page 143). It also goes well with turkey, pork, and meatloaf.

1. Preheat the oven to 400 degrees.

2. Toss the yams with the oil and salt, arrange in a single layer in a baking dish, and roast at 400 degrees for 15 minutes.

3. Remove from the oven and toss with the lime juice and/or lime slices and the maple syrup.

4. Roast for another 15 minutes.

5. Remove from the oven and toss with the pecans and coconut.

6. Bake for about 5 more minutes or until the coconut is toasted and the yams are soft.

Serves 2–4

2 cups cubed yams or sweet potatoes, peeled

1 Tbs. coconut oil

½ tsp. salt or salt substitute

1 Tbs. fresh lime juice (and/or thin slices of key lime)

1 Tbs. maple syrup

¼ cup chopped pecans

¼ cup shredded coconut

BENEFITS Yams (and/or sweet potatoes) contain carotenoids and fiber. Carotenoids inhibit cancer and tumor growth, reduce your risk of heart disease, and support immune function. Fiber lowers blood cholesterol and, like carotenoids, reduces your risk of heart disease.

Atchara Pickle

When I was a teenager in the Philippines, my mom and I would make atchara. This sweet-and-sour pickle is made with green, unripe papayas and other vegetables. My mom made carrot florets to add beauty and color to the pickle. Eaten with grilled pork or fried fish, atchara is considered a national dish of the Philippines. In America, I eat it with BBQ, grilled meat, and smoked fish.

1. Place the papaya in a colander and sprinkle with the coarse salt. Allow to sit for 15 minutes.

2. Make the pickling solution: Combine the vinegar, sugar, and salt in a porcelain or glass pan (don't use a metal pot). Simmer for 10 minutes or until all the sugar has dissolved. Remove from the heat and allow to cool.

3. Squeeze any remaining water out of the papaya. Toss with the remaining ingredients and distribute among wide-mouth pickling jars.

4. Pour the pickling solution over the vegetables. Top off the jars with water if necessary so that the vegetables are completely covered. Close the jars tightly and refrigerate overnight to cure.

CHEF'S NOTE *If you prefer to use white vinegar or apple cider vinegar instead of white balsamic vinegar, cut it with an equal amount of water or it will be too harsh. The amount of sugar in this recipe makes a sour pickle. For a sweet-and-sour pickle, double the amount of sugar. Be sure to cool the pickling solution; if it's too warm, the vegetables will cook.*

Serves 8–10

8 cups coarsely grated green papaya (or cucumbers)

¼ cup coarse salt

3 cups white balsamic vinegar (or champagne vinegar or seasoned rice vinegar)

¾ cup white or natural sugar

2 tsp. salt or salt substitute

½ cup peeled pearl onions

½ cup red bell pepper strips

½ cup green bell pepper strips

½ cup carrot florets or strips

½ cup jicama strips

¼ cup julienned ginger

8–10 peeled garlic cloves

BENEFITS Papayas contain papain, an enzyme that helps break down proteins. I sometimes use green papaya as a meat tenderizer. Papaya and jicama are rich in fiber, which helps regulate cholesterol and aids in weight loss. Vinegar can lower blood sugar and may help with weight loss because it helps you feel more full and satisfied.

Citrusy Asparagus

Asparagus is a finicky vegetable. It must be very fresh and picked early in the season or it will have woody stalks. Don't cut the dry ends off of the stalks. Instead, bend the stalks until the dry ends break off. Otherwise you risk serving chewy, inedible asparagus parts that your guests won't enjoy. This citrusy side dish can be served hot or cold and is good cut up and served in a salad.

1. Blanch the asparagus in a large pot of boiling water for 5–7 minutes or until tender. Drain and plunge into an ice bath. Pat dry with a paper towel.

2. If serving cold: Wrap the spears in a paper towel to retain moisture and chill in the refrigerator for up to 4 hours. Then whisk the remaining ingredients together in a small bowl and toss with the chilled spears.

3. If serving warm: Whisk the orange juice, lemon juice, and salt and toss with the asparagus. Sauté the garlic and ginger in the oil over medium heat for 3 minutes. Add the spears and sauté for 2–3 more minutes or until the asparagus is heated through. Season with the salt and serve.

Serves 4–6

2 lbs. asparagus spears, ends snapped off

4 Tbs. orange juice

1 Tbs. fresh lemon juice

½ tsp. sea salt or salt substitute

4 Tbs. olive oil

1 tsp. grated ginger

1 tsp. minced garlic

CHEF'S NOTE *You can start this recipe a day or so ahead of time. After blanching the asparagus, wrap them in a paper towel to retain moisture and refrigerate until you are ready to complete the recipe.*

BENEFITS Asparagus has lycopene and vitamin C. Lycopene is an antioxidant that lowers cancer risk, aids cognitive function, and promotes prostate health. Vitamin C helps the body resist infection, prevent cataracts, and regenerate tissue.

Mushroom Medley

Mushrooms detoxify the soil they grow in. This side dish pairs well with chicken, beef, or game meats. You can use almost any variety of mushroom in any combination. I leave the small mushrooms whole because they look nicer that way, but you can chop them if you prefer.

1. In a heavy enamel-covered pan, braise the mushrooms in the butter and garlic over low to medium heat for 10–15 minutes, stirring often, or until the mushrooms shrink and darken all the way through.

2. Add the balsamic vinegar, herbs, salt, and pepper and cook for 5–10 minutes or until the liquid has thickened a bit.

CHEF'S NOTE *If you use dried mushrooms, first hydrate them in boiling-hot water for at least 20 minutes, then drain well before braising.*

Serves 2–4

1 cup shiitake mushrooms

1 cup white button mushrooms

1 cup chopped Portobello mushrooms

1 cup cremini mushrooms

3 Tbs. butter

1 tsp. minced garlic

1 Tbs. balsamic vinegar

1 tsp. fresh chopped parsley

1 tsp. fresh chopped oregano

1 tsp. fresh chopped thyme

1 tsp. fresh chopped marjoram

¼ sea salt or salt substitute

¼ tsp. black pepper

BENEFITS Mushrooms contain selenium, an antioxidant that boosts immune function and reduces cancer risk. Beta glucans in mushrooms boost the immune system. Mushrooms are also a good source of vitamin D for strong bones.

Stuffed Sugar Pumpkins

Sugar pumpkins are mostly used as decoration in the fall months. That's a shame because they are the best variety of pumpkin to cook with. Their flesh is less stringy and watery than the larger jack-o'-lantern pumpkins. I like to roast them for a nice holiday side dish.

1. Preheat the oven to 350 degrees.

2. Prepare the pumpkins: Carefully remove the top of each pumpkin, scoop out the seeds and fibers with a spoon, and clean the pumpkin tops. Discard the seeds and fibers.

3. Salt and pepper the cavity of each pumpkin.

4. Spoon the applesauce into the cavity of each pumpkin. Depending on the size of the pumpkin, you will use anywhere from ¼ cup to 1 cup of applesauce per pumpkin. Fill the pumpkin to just beneath the top rim.

5. Replace the pumpkin tops and roast in the oven at 350 degrees for 45 minutes to 1 hour or until the pumpkins are tender but not mushy.

Serves 4–6

4–6 sugar pumpkins

Salt or salt substitute and freshly ground black pepper to taste

About 4 cups applesauce

BENEFITS Pumpkins contain cucurbitacin, a steroid-like anti-inflammatory compound that may inhibit cancer cells. They are also loaded with carotenoids, which enhance the appearance of the skin and are converted in the body into immune-boosting vitamin A.

Cauliflower Steaks with Herbed Goat Cheese

These cauliflower steaks can serve as a vegetarian main course or sit beautifully alongside grass-fed, grilled rib eye or Porterhouse steaks. Piment d'Espelette is the French version of paprika. It's mild and full-flavored. You can use paprika or red pepper flakes (1 tsp.) instead.

1. Preheat the oven to 400 degrees.

2. Spread the olive oil in a large baking dish and lay the cauliflower slices in a single layer in the dish.

3. Dot with the butter pieces and sprinkle with half of the seasonings.

4. Roast at 400 degrees for 20 minutes.

5. Turn the cauliflower over, sprinkle with the remaining seasonings, and roast another 20 minutes or until tender.

6. Allow the cauliflower to cool slightly. Place on a serving tray and dot with the goat cheese. Garnish with the chives.

CHEF'S NOTE *While slicing the cauliflower, some of the slices will fall apart. That's okay.*

Serves 4–6

2 Tbs. olive oil

1 head cauliflower, cut into 1-inch slices

1 Tbs. butter, cut into small pieces

1 tsp. piment d'Espelette, divided in half

Salt or salt substitute and freshly ground black pepper to taste

4–5 oz. herbed goat cheese spread

1 Tbs. fresh chopped chives, as garnish

BENEFITS Cauliflower has indoles (sulfur compounds), which help to prevent cancer by neutralizing carcinogens. It also contains SOD (superoxide dismutase), an antioxidant and anti-inflammatory that fights free-radical damage in your cells and keeps skin youthful-looking.

Coconut-Lemongrass Rice

Coconut rice is easy to make, good for you, and delicious. It goes well with my Beer-Basted Chicken (page 123). I like to cook the rice with banana leaves, which impart a little bit of flavor and help keep the rice from scorching the bottom of the pot, but you can omit them. If you can't find fresh lemongrass, use ½ Tbs. lemongrass stir-in paste or zest from ½ lemon instead.

Serves 2–4

1 cup jasmine rice

1 stalk lemongrass

2 banana leaves

1 cup water

1 cup canned light or regular coconut milk

½ tsp. sea salt

1. Rinse the rice twice in clean water.
2. Cut the lemongrass stalk (white part only) into 3 pieces and pound them with a mallet a few times.
3. Line the bottom of the rice pot with the banana leaves.
4. Add the lemongrass, rice, water, coconut milk, and salt. Bring to a boil and simmer, covered, for 20–25 minutes or until the rice is tender. Add more water if needed.
5. Before serving, remove the lemongrass and discard.

BENEFITS Coconut milk has protein and lauric acid, an anti-inflammatory fat that can improve your cholesterol balance and prostate health. Lemongrass contains citral, which, when applied topically, has been shown to induce cancer cells to kill themselves.

desserts

Raspberry-Cream Banana Splits

Here's a rich, creamy frozen dessert that's vegan. This heart-healthy confection delivers decadent coolness without any animal fats. I also use coconut cream—not to be confused with coconut milk or sweetened cream of coconut. Coconut cream is thicker and heavier than coconut milk and usually comes unsweetened in cans or Tetra Packs. Even the chocolate sauce is vegan.

1. Make the raspberry-cashew cream: Place the cashews in a small bowl. Cover with the warm water and soak for 1 hour. While they are soaking, purée the raspberries and the cold water until smooth, then strain the seeds out. Drain the cashews and blend them with the raspberries, lemon zest, and coconut cream until smooth. Pour into ice cube trays and freeze for 4–5 hours or until hard.

2. Make the sauce: Whisk together the cocoa powder, agave syrup, and coconut milk until smooth. Chill until ready to use.

3. Just before serving, blend the cubes of raspberry-cashew "ice" cream in the blender until thick and smooth.

4. To serve, slice the bananas lengthwise and divide the slices between two serving dishes. Top with scoops of the "ice" cream, then the chocolate sauce and chopped walnuts.

CHEF'S NOTE *I like to use Trader Joe's brand of coconut milk and coconut cream.*

Serves 2

1 cup raw cashews

Warm water to cover

1 cup very ripe raspberries

½ cup cold water

½ tsp. lemon zest

3 Tbs. coconut cream

2 Tbs. cocoa powder

2 Tbs. agave syrup

2–3 Tbs. coconut milk

2 peeled bananas

¼ cup chopped walnuts

BENEFITS Coconut cream contains lauric acid, an anti-inflammatory that can improve your cholesterol balance and prostate health. The monounsaturated fats in cashews are anti-inflammatory and can improve the appearance of the skin. Raspberries are loaded with vitamin C, which helps the body resist infection, aids tissue regeneration, and helps prevent cataracts.

IB

M

Jujube Crumble

When jujubes are still green and unwrinkled, they taste just like tart Granny Smith apples. As they ripen, they wrinkle and turn a dark reddish-brown color. They also become much sweeter than apples. You can use Granny Smith or other green apples instead. Freshly grated nutmeg and lemon zest make all the difference in this homey crumble, made with oat flour, nuts, and a bit of cheese for extra oomph.

1. Preheat the oven to 350 degrees.

2. Cut the jujubes into quarters, removing stems and seeds. Toss with the ¼ cup of sugar, lemon juice, and lemon zest. Place in a 9-inch glass pie plate or distribute among 4 small ramekins or ceramic baking dishes.

3. Make the crumble: In a large glass or ceramic bowl, blend the crumble ingredients with your fingertips until the mixture resembles coarse meal.

4. Spread the mixture evenly over the jujubes and bake in the oven at 350 degrees for 15–30 minutes or until the top is brown and crisp.

CHEF'S NOTE *If the jujubes are dark reddish-brown, wrinkled, and fully ripened, leave out the first ¼ cup of sugar. If you can't find oat flour, pulverize rolled oats in a food mill or food processor, or use whole-wheat flour instead.*

Serves 8

6 cups unripe green jujubes

¼ cup raw or all-natural brown sugar

1 Tbs. fresh lemon juice

2 tsp. lemon zest

Crumble

1 cup oat flour

½ cup rolled oats

½ cup grated cheddar or Parmesan cheese

½ cup raw or all-natural brown sugar

½ cup chopped walnuts

⅓ cup cubed chilled butter or Smart Balance

1 tsp. lemon zest

½ tsp. ground cinnamon

¼ tsp. freshly grated nutmeg

BENEFITS Jujubes are a traditional remedy for anxiety and sleeplessness. They're also a good source of vitamin C, which helps the body resist infection. Preliminary animal research suggests that the antioxidants in jujubes may help protect the brain and boost memory. Walnuts are a good source of Omega-3s, which help ward off depression.

Sweet Mung Beans

I based this dish on Chinese mung bean soup, which is traditionally served at the end of multicourse banquet meals. It can also be eaten as a sweet appetizer. The sweetened agar-agar cubes (similar to gelatin cubes) add brightness and a fun texture. Made from seaweed, agar-agar is a vegetarian alternative to gelatin. If you can't find agar-agar powder, you can use gelatin powder instead. Red mung beans can be difficult to find, but they make the prettiest soup. The green variety will work in a pinch. This dish can be served hot or cold.

1. Boil the agar-agar powder or bar in the cup of water for 5–8 minutes or until the agar-agar dissolves fully and the mixture becomes transparent.

2. Remove from the heat and stir in the agave syrup. Pour into a rectangular or square glass pan (up to 8 x 8 inches) and chill for at least an hour. When firm, cut into ¼-inch cubes. Chill until ready to serve.

3. Simmer the rice in the coconut milk for 25–35 minutes or until tender. Set aside.

4. Cook the mung beans in the 4 cups of water for 30–45 minutes or until soft. Allow to cool without draining the water. Blend or mash with the cooking water until smooth.

5. Fold the cooked tapioca into the beans and keep warm over low heat. Add the rice and warm through for 5–10 minutes. Add the agave syrup to the sweetness you desire.

6. To serve, pour into bowls and top with the agar-agar cubes.

Serves 8–10

½ cup agar-agar powder (or a long bar of agar-agar soaked in a little water for 30 min. and drained)

1 cup water

¼ cup agave syrup

⅓ cup wild rice

1 cup coconut milk

1 cup small red mung beans, soaked overnight

4 cups water

⅓ cup cooked tapioca (instant or regular)

½–1 cup agave syrup

CHEF'S NOTE *You can find agar-agar powder at a variety of online sources and agar-agar bars at Eden Organic, edenfoods.com.*

BENEFITS Mung beans are an excellent source of folate, a nutrient that reduces the risk of certain cancers and heart disease. They're also a good source of fiber, which helps lower cholesterol and lowers your risk of certain types of cancer. Wild rice contains anthyocyanins, which have antioxidant properties.

Stuffed Peaches

A simple plate of ripe fruit can make a nice dessert, but I don't lean toward simple. I like my desserts to be fabulous! These stuffed peaches take cut fruit to a new level. The nuts and the coconut add health and beauty benefits. Since they can be eaten by hand, these peaches make wonderful tray-passed party food. To make this recipe vegan, use maple syrup instead of honey.

1. Cut the peaches in half and remove the pits.

2. With a melon baller, scoop out about 1 Tbs. peach flesh from the center of each peach. You will have a hole about twice the size of the one left from the pit.

3. Cover the peaches with plastic wrap and refrigerate.

4. In a food processor, blend the peach pulp and the remaining ingredients (except the garnishes) for a few seconds until you get a chunky, uniform mixture.

5. Freeze for 1–2 hours.

6. To serve, fill each peach half with the frozen mixture using a small ice cream scooper or tablespoon. Garnish with toasted coconut and walnuts or almonds.

CHEF'S NOTE *If your peaches aren't perfectly ripe, quickly grill them before stuffing them. This will bring out their sugars and soften their fibers. Just brush the cut sides with melted coconut oil and grill over high heat for 2–3 minutes.*

Serves 4–8

4 ripe medium-sized peaches

1 cup shredded coconut

½ cup almonds (raw or roasted)

½ cup cashews (raw or roasted)

2–3 Tbs. honey

2 Tbs. fresh lemon juice

1 tsp. lemon zest

¼ tsp. salt

½ cup toasted coconut, as garnish

½ cup walnuts or slivered almonds, as garnish

BENEFITS Peaches contain carotenoids, which your body needs to produce vitamin A, a beauty-enhancing antioxidant that keeps eyes healthy and boosts immune function. The monounsaturated fats in almonds and cashews contribute to youthful looking skin. Coconut's lauric acid helps balance cholesterol levels.

Banana Citrus Cake

My friend Ossie inspired this excellent cake. I bake it in a loaf pan, but you can also use a Bundt pan.

1. Preheat the oven to 350 degrees. Grease a loaf pan and line it with parchment paper.

2. In a stand mixer, beat the flour, sugar, baking powder, and baking soda for 30 seconds.

3. In a separate bowl, whisk together the bananas, orange juice, butter, and eggs. Pour into the flour mixture and beat at medium speed for 3 minutes.

4. Fold in the walnuts, cranberries, and chocolate chips.

5. Pour the batter into the loaf pan and bake at 350 degrees for 35–50 minutes or until a toothpick inserted into the middle of the loaf comes out clean.

6. Cool for at least 1 hour. Slice and serve.

Serves 8–12

2¼ cups all-purpose flour

1 cup raw or demerara sugar

2½ tsp. baking powder

½ tsp. baking soda

½ cup mashed banana

1 cup orange juice

½ cup melted butter or Smart Balance

2 eggs (organic, free-range, or Omega-3-enriched)

½ cup walnut pieces

¼ cup dried cranberries

¼ cup semisweet chocolate chips

BENEFITS Bananas have potassium, which helps regulate blood pressure. Orange juice contains vitamin C, which helps protect skin from aging. Walnuts are a good source of anti-inflammatory Omega-3 fatty acids.

Mini Cheddar-Rice Cupcakes

These cupcakes are both sweet and a little bit savory—a classic flavor combination in Southeast Asia, where I grew up. My American friends usually haven't encountered cupcakes like these before, but once they taste them, they're hooked.

1. Preheat the oven to 350 degrees.

2. In a large mixing bowl, combine the flours, xylitol or sugar, and baking powder. Stir until the mixture is uniform.

3. Gradually whisk in the milk until the mixture is smooth, and add the vanilla.

4. Strain the batter and pour into nonstick mini-cupcake pans, filling them halfway (or ¾ at most). Top each with a pinch of cheddar cheese.

5. Place the pans inside a larger baking dish or roasting pan. Fill with hot water until it reaches halfway up the sides of the cupcake pans.

6. Bake at 350 degrees for 20 minutes. The cupcakes will rise dramatically. They don't need to brown on top.

7. Remove the pans from the oven and place on a cooling rack for about 20 minutes. Lift out the cupcakes with a small spatula.

Yields 24 mini-cupcakes

1 cup rice flour

1 cup cake flour

1 cup xylitol or sugar

4 tsp. baking powder

2 cups low-fat milk

¼ tsp. vanilla

½ cup grated low-fat cheddar cheese

BENEFITS Rice flour is a good source of the antioxidant mineral selenium and a particularly good source of manganese, which helps build strong bones. Milk and cheddar cheese provide protein and calcium for strong bones and muscles.

Baobab Butter Squares

These squares are like lemon bars but made with antioxidant-rich baobab. You can use fresh lemon juice (3 Tbs.) or lemon zest (1 Tbs.) instead of the baobab powder and substitute gluten-free flour for the wheat-based flour.

1. Preheat the oven to 325 degrees.

2. Make the crust: In a stand mixer, combine the crust ingredients and mix on low speed until well blended. Spread evenly in an 8 x 8-inch baking pan. Press down evenly in the center with your fingers, but let the edges rise up along the sides of the pan just a bit, almost like a tart shell.

3. Bake at 325 degrees for 15–20 minutes or until golden brown on top. The crust won't be completely done.

4. Make the filling: In a large glass mixing bowl, whisk the filling ingredients. Don't whip or overbeat.

5. Pour the filling over the partially baked crust. Return to the oven for another 20 minutes or until the filling is set (when you shake the pan, the filling should jiggle and hold, not run like water).

6. Allow to cool for at least 20 minutes.

7. Garnish with the powdered sugar. Cut into squares and serve.

CHEF'S NOTE *I have used Baobest baobab fruit powder, but there are now organic baobab powders on the market. They are all available on Amazon.com.*

Yields 12 squares

Crust

½ cup butter, softened

1⅓ cups all-purpose flour

¼ cup xylitol or white sugar

¼ tsp. salt or salt substitute

Filling

2 eggs (organic, free-range, or Omega-3-enriched)

¾ cup xylitol or white sugar

4 Tbs. baobab powder

2 Tbs. all-purpose flour

2 tsp. lemon zest

1 tsp. baking powder

Garnish

2–4 Tbs. powdered sugar

BENEFITS Baobab is a good source of vitamin C, an antioxidant that appears to guard against heart disease and stroke and also protects the skin from the aging effects of ultraviolet rays. It contains fiber, which helps with digestion and gut health.

Rice and Corn Pudding

Here's my fun twist on rice pudding. The wild rice and corn give it a much more interesting texture and lots of health benefits. Many forms of coconut are used to make this pudding, from coconut milk to coconut cream and even coconut oil. Coconut cream is thicker and heavier than coconut milk. When you buy it sweetened, it's called cream of coconut. If you can't find coconut cream, you can omit it. This is a rich, delicious dessert that I serve in small portions.

1. Rinse the jasmine rice twice and place in a glass or ceramic pan with 4 cups of the coconut milk.

2. Bring to a boil, reduce heat, and simmer, covered, for 20–30 minutes, stirring occasionally, or until the rice has a porridge-like consistency.

3. Add the corn kernels and cook for another 10–15 minutes, or until the rice and corn are fully cooked.

4. Remove from the heat and add the coconut cream, honey, and 2 Tbs. of the coconut oil.

5. While the jasmine rice is cooking, toast the wild rice in a saucepan over medium heat for about 5 minutes, stirring frequently.

6. Add the remaining coconut milk and simmer for 20 minutes or until the rice is crunchy outside and tender inside.

7. Remove from the heat and add the remaining coconut oil.

8. Dish up the pudding into individual bowls. Top with the wild rice mixture.

CHEF'S NOTE *If you use sweetened coconut cream, omit the honey. You can use frozen corn if you don't have fresh corn.*

Serves 10–12

½ cup jasmine rice

5 cups coconut milk

2 cups fresh corn kernels, removed from cob

1 cup coconut cream

½ cup honey

4 Tbs. coconut oil, divided in half

¼ cup wild rice

BENEFITS Coconut milk is high in lauric acid, an anti-inflammatory fatty acid that can improve your cholesterol balance. Wild rice contains anthocyanins, which may reduce your risk of heart disease and enhance cognitive function.

Macadamia Cream Flan

My dairy-free Macadamia Cream is very decadent tasting and smooth. I use organic, free-range, or Omega-3-enriched eggs for added benefits. You can use almonds or cashews instead of macadamia nuts.

1. Preheat the oven to 375 degrees.

2. Make the caramel: In a small saucepan, combine the water and xylitol or sugar and cook over medium heat for 8–10 minutes or until the mixture bubbles and turns golden brown. Do not stir!

3. Remove from the heat and pour into two flan molds or 4–6 ramekins. Tilt the molds or ramekins to evenly distribute the caramel along the bottom.

4. Make the flan: In a large mixing bowl, whisk the egg yolks and the whole egg for about 5 minutes. Add the Macadamia Cream, xylitol or sugar, and lemon zest. Whisk for another 5 minutes.

5. Strain the flan into the caramel-bottomed flan molds or ramekins.

6. Place the molds in a large baking dish and fill the dish ⅓ of the way with hot water. Cover the molds with aluminum foil and bake at 375 degrees for 1 hour.

7. Remove the foil and bake another 10–15 minutes or until the flan sets.

8. Remove the molds from the baking dish. Allow to cool for 20 minutes, then chill in the refrigerator for at least 2 hours.

9. Run a knife around the inside edge of one mold or ramekin. Invert the flan onto a small plate and serve immediately. Repeat with the remaining molds or ramekins.

Yields 8 small servings

Caramel

½ cup water

1 cup xylitol or sugar

Flan

8 egg yolks (organic, free-range, or Omega-3-enriched)

1 egg (organic, free-range, or Omega-3-enriched)

2 cups Macadamia Cream (page 243)

⅔ cup xylitol or sugar

1 tsp. lemon zest

CHEF'S NOTE *To turn this flan into a crème brûlée, omit the caramel and begin with step 3. Bake the flan in ramekins, not in flan molds. Cool the flan as usual. After cooling, remove the flan from the refrigerator and sprinkle the top of each ramekin with 2 Tbs. granulated sugar. Using a kitchen torch, burn the sugar until it is brown and glassy. Allow the crème brûlée to cool slightly before serving.*

BENEFITS Macadamia nuts are rich in heart-healthy, anti-inflammatory monounsaturated fats. Eating more of these healthy fats can help keep your skin youthful and your waistline trim. Egg yolks contain lutein, which reduces the risk of cataracts and age-related macular degeneration.

Strawberry-Banana Sorbet

A bright, refreshing sorbet is perfect on a summer evening. My ice-cream maker allows me to whip up a frozen dessert whenever I want it. You may have to freeze the bowl of your ice-cream maker overnight, so check the instructions before you start this recipe. You can use blueberries, oranges, mangoes, or other fruit instead of the strawberries.

1. In a small saucepan, bring the xylitol or sugar and water to a boil over medium heat.

2. Add the kumquat slices, reduce the heat to low, and simmer for about 15 minutes or until the liquid is reduced by half.

3. Strain and reserve the syrup.

4. In a blender, purée the strawberries, banana, and lemon juice.

5. Add the syrup and blend for a few seconds. In the blender cup, chill the mixture in the refrigerator for about 1 hour.

6. Remove from the refrigerator and put the blender cup back on its base. Add the egg white and blend for 30 seconds.

7. Pour into an ice-cream maker and process for about 20–30 minutes or according to manufacturer's directions for sorbet. Serve immediately or transfer to a plastic container, cover the surface of the sorbet with plastic wrap to keep ice crystals from forming, and freeze for a few hours.

Serves 6–8

¼ cup xylitol or sugar (or 1 Tbs. plus 2 tsp. Truvia)

1 cup water

½ cup sliced kumquats

3 cups strawberries, hulls removed

2 cups banana chunks

2 tsp. fresh lemon juice

1 egg white (organic, free-range, or Omega-3-enriched)

BENEFITS Strawberries and kumquats are very high in vitamin C, a well-known immunity booster. Bananas contain potassium, which supports nerve and muscle function and reduces the risk of osteoporosis and even kidney stones.

Coconut-Rice Cake

Eat this chewy cake warm. It's great plain or drizzled with my berry sauce for extra antioxidant power. Be sure to use the chewy variety of rice flour sometimes called sweet white rice flour or mochiko. You can substitute fresh or frozen blackberries for the boysenberries. You can use gluten-free baking flour instead of the cake flour.

1. Preheat the oven to 375 degrees.

2. In a stand mixer, begin beating the eggs while gradually adding the xylitol or sugar. Keep beating until the eggs get foamy and the sugar is fully dissolved. It will look like a meringue.

3. In a separate bowl, mix the cake flour, rice flour, and baking powder. Fold in the milks, then the meringue, then the oil.

4. Line one pie pan with parchment paper. Spread the batter evenly over the parchment paper and bake for 30 minutes or until the top turns golden brown and a toothpick inserted in the center of the cake comes out clean.

5. Make the berry sauce: While the cake is baking, combine all the berry sauce ingredients in a small saucepan and cook over medium heat for 5–10 minutes or until the berries give up some of their liquid.

6. When the cake is finished baking, allow it to cool slightly. Remove it from the pan and sprinkle it with the shredded coconut (if using). Serve with the berry sauce on the side.

Serves 6–8

2 eggs (organic, free-range, or Omega-3-enriched)

½ cup xylitol or sugar

½ cup cake flour

½ cup glutinous rice flour

2½ tsp. baking powder

½ cup coconut milk

3 Tbs. low-fat milk

3 Tbs. vegetable oil

Berry sauce

½ cup fresh boysenberries or blackberries

⅛ cup sliced kumquats (optional)

⅛ cup honey or maple syrup

½ Tbs. fresh lemon juice

¼ tsp. lemon zest

Garnish

1–1½ Tbs. shredded coconut (optional)

BENEFITS Coconut contains lauric acid, which improves cholesterol balance and protects prostate health. Berries are full of anthocyanins, which inhibit the growth of cancer cells.

Dark Chocolate Mousse

It's hard to imagine, but this tofu version of a chocolate mousse offers the same satisfaction as its richer, less healthy sibling. Contributed by my colleague Dr. Lynn Blair, it has all the same creaminess, the satiny, melt-in-your-mouth pleasure, and the full, no-holds-barred taste you expect from a dense and rich chocolate mousse.

1. In the top of a double boiler, melt the chocolate, cocoa powder, milk, water, vanilla extract, liqueur, and xylitol or sugar, stirring constantly until the chocolate is fully melted.

2. Remove from the heat and stir in the honey. Set aside.

3. Blend the tofu in a food processor for 2–3 minutes or until very smooth.

4. Fold the tofu into the chocolate mixture.

5. Spoon the mousse into serving bowls and chill in the refrigerator for at least 3 hours.

6. Garnish with the sliced kumquats.

Serves 4

8 oz. high-quality dark chocolate, broken into pieces

¼ cup unsweetened cocoa powder

1 Tbs. soy or almond milk

¼ cup water

⅛ tsp. vanilla extract

2 Tbs. Grand Marnier liqueur

¼ cup xylitol or sugar

¼ cup honey

1 package (9–10 oz.) or 1¼ cups silken tofu, well drained

½ cup sliced kumquats, as garnish

BENEFITS Soy contains isoflavones, which help preserve bone density, lower your risk of certain cancers, and may alleviate menopausal symptoms. Dark chocolate has catechins, which are neuroprotective, and theobromine, which improves blood flow and lowers blood pressure.

Moringa Chiffon Muffins

Moringa leaves, in their powdered form, give these muffins their distinctive green color and healthful benefits.

1. Preheat the oven to 350 degrees.

2. Moringa water: Mix the moringa powder in the warm water until smooth. Set aside and let cool for about 15 minutes.

3. Dry-ingredients mixture: In a large glass bowl combine the dry ingredients and mix well. Push the mixture up along the sides of the bowl and create a hole in the center, making a well.

4. Egg-yolk mixture: Pour the egg-yolk mixture ingredients into the well. Starting in the center, slowly whisk the liquid ingredients together and then whisk in the dry ingredients until you have a batter that is smooth. Set aside.

5. Egg-white mixture: Pour the egg-white mixture ingredients except the sugar into a stand mixer and beat on high speed about 4–6 minutes or until foamy. Gradually add the sugar and continue beating another 3–5 minutes or until stiff peaks form.

6. Using a big rubber spatula, gently fold the egg-white mixture into the batter until it is a uniform color. Divide evenly into muffin pans lined with 24 cupcake paper liners, filling the papers about ¾ full.

7. Bake for 12–15 minutes or until a toothpick inserted in the center of a muffin comes out clean. Place the muffin pans on a cooling rack and allow to cool.

Yields 24 muffins

Moringa water

½ cup lukewarm water

2 tsp. moringa powder

Dry-ingredients mixture

1 cup + 2 Tbs. cake flour, sifted

6 Tbs. sugar

1½ tsp. baking powder

Egg-yolk mixture

5 egg yolks (unbeaten)

¼ cup corn oil

1 tsp. vanilla extract

½ tsp. natural green food color

Cooled moringa water

Egg-white mixture

5 egg whites

½ tsp. cream of tartar

¼ tsp. sea salt

6 Tbs. sugar

BENEFITS Moringa contains quercetin and other flavonoids that can help protect your liver; thiocarbamate glycosides, nitrile, and mustard oil glycosides that help stabilize blood pressure; and B-sitosterol that helps lower cholesterol. It is a good source of protein, minerals (calcium, iron, magnesium, nitrate, potassium), and vitamins A and C.

Seasonal Fruit Upside-Down Cake

This gluten-free recipe is so versatile, you can use just about any fresh fruit and it will taste wonderful. I've used blueberries, plums, pears, apples, peaches, mangoes, and even cherries. You can also use all-purpose flour instead of gluten-free. This cake can be served warm or cool.

1. Preheat the oven to 350 degrees.

2. In a saucepan or 10-inch cast-iron skillet, melt the butter over medium heat. Add the sugar, stir, and cook for 2–3 minutes or until well mixed.

3. Pour the mixture into a 10-inch round cake pan (or leave in skillet if ovenproof) and spread evenly with a spatula.

4. Lay the fresh fruit over the mixture evenly and set the pan aside.

5. In a large mixing bowl, mix the flours, baking powder, and salt and set aside.

6. In a stand mixer with paddle attachment, beat the xylitol or sugar and butter until fluffy. Mix in the vanilla extract. Blend in the eggs one at a time. Gradually add the flour mixture and blend thoroughly. Slowly fold in the yogurt.

7. Spoon the batter evenly over the fruit in the cake pan and bake on the middle oven rack at 350 degrees for 40–45 minutes or until a toothpick inserted in the center comes out clean.

Continued on next page

Serves 10–12

½ cup (1 stick) unsalted butter

½ cup light brown sugar

2 cups fresh seasonal fruit

1 cup gluten-free baking flour

½ cup almond flour

½ cup coconut flour

1 Tbs. baking powder

1 tsp. salt or salt substitute

1½ cups xylitol or sugar

1 cup cubed, slightly softened unsalted butter

2 tsp. vanilla extract

4 large eggs (organic, free-range, or Omega-3-enriched), separated

¾ cup plain yogurt

BENEFITS Blueberries are full of antioxidants, most notably anthocyanins, which improve blood flow to capillaries, helping the brain and skin to be healthy. Almond flour and eggs both add choline, which helps balance your brain chemistry. The almond flour also contributes vitamin E for beautiful skin, hair, and nails and for healthy brain function.

Seasonal Fruit
Upside-Down Cake

Continued from previous page

8. Allow to cool for 10–15 minutes. Run a knife along the inside edge of the cake pan while it is still warm to loosen it.

9. Cover the cake pan with a plate or large tray and turn it upside-down to invert the cake onto the plate.

CHEF'S NOTE *If you're using another type of fresh fruit, be sure to peel, slice, and de-seed it if needed. The slices should be about ¼-inch thick.*

drinks

Coconut Slushie

Refreshment doesn't come any creamier than this. My coconut slushie uses frozen young coconut meat. Coconut water is available in many grocery stores these days. The raw, unpasteurized version tastes the best. You can use heavy coconut milk instead of coconut meat, but the texture will be different.

Serves 2

**1 fresh coconut or
½ package (8 oz.) frozen
raw coconut meat**

2 cups coconut water

2 cups ice

2–3 Tbs. honey

Place all the ingredients in a blender and whirl about 5 minutes or until smooth.

CHEF'S NOTE *You can find raw coconut meat at Asian and specialty markets and at Exotic Superfoods: exoticsuperfoods.com*

BENEFITS Coconut is a wonderful food. It has protein, medium-chain fatty acids that are especially easy for your body to break down and convert to energy, and lauric acid, an anti-inflammatory that can improve your cholesterol balance and prostate health.

Jujube Tea

Jujube trees grow in China and the Middle East, where they are enjoyed for their shade and their sweet fruit. The fruits are sometimes called Chinese dates or Indian dates. In America, we eat a candy based on their sweet flavor. In Asia, the fruit is often dried and made into a tea. Jujube tea is used in homeopathic medicine to calm nerves and soothe sore throats, and acts as a laxative. It doesn't need a sweetener because the fruit is naturally sweet. You can boil fresh or dried jujubes as long as they're ripe. You can serve this tea hot or chilled.

Serves 4

1 cup dried jujubes

5 cups water

Boil the jujubes in the water for 10–20 minutes or until the color of the water turns a deep reddish-brown. Strain and serve.

CHEF'S NOTE *To dry jujubes: Place 10 jujubes in a tray in a 100-degree oven for 8–10 hours, turning occasionally, or put the jujubes in indirect sunlight for 5–7 days or until they are wrinkled and brown. Fresh jujubes are available in the fall. You can find jujubes online at Melissa's: melissas.com.*

BENEFITS Jujubes contain vitamin C, which boosts immunity by helping the body resist infection. Preliminary research suggests that the antioxidants in jujubes may help protect the brain and enhance memory.

Thinkstock Photo by habovka

Beet, Orange, and Watercress Juice

I like to think of this as a detox juice. The beets help sweeten the juice and give it a beautiful color. If you can't get fresh watercress, you can use spirulina powder instead.

Serves 2–3

1 cup watercress (or 2 Tbs. spirulina powder)

4 beets (peels on, stems and roots removed), cut in pieces

4 oranges, cut in pieces

2 Tbs. fiber powder

1 cup water

1. Run the watercress, beets, and oranges through a juicer. Pour the juice into a pitcher.

2. Stir the fiber powder into the water until it dissolves completely.

3. Mix the fiber water into the juice until fully incorporated.

CHEF'S NOTE *Some people can't tolerate orange peel, which adds a spicy undertone to this drink. If you prefer, peel the oranges first.*

BENEFITS The chlorophyll in watercress helps deactivate carcinogenic compounds. Beets contain disease-preventing anthocyanins, as well as natural nitrates, which moderate blood pressure. The vitamin C in the oranges is a powerful antioxidant. And the fiber powder helps keep your colon healthy.

Thinkstock Photo by poplasen

Mind and Beauty Juice

This juice blend is specifically formulated to help the skin look young and beautiful while protecting the mind. I use my Blendtec® Tabletop Total Blender to pulverize the carrots, cantaloupe, and cucumber.

Serves 2
1 bag (16 oz.) organic baby carrots
½ cantaloupe, rind removed, seeded, and cut in pieces
1 cucumber, peeled, seeded, and cut in pieces
1 egg white (organic, free-range, or Omega-3-enriched), beaten
1 cup cold green tea

1. Juice the carrots, cantaloupe, and cucumber.

2. Mix with the beaten egg white and tea.

BENEFITS Carrots and melons have carotenoids, an antioxidant that fights skin aging. Cucumbers are a good source of vitamin K, building strong bones and protecting the heart. Egg white provides protein for building muscles, bones, and blood, and the catechins in green tea help keep teeth cavity-free and brains sharp.

Honey-Lemongrass Tea

Lemongrass tea is a classic Southeast Asian staple. In my recipe, I pair lemongrass with natural, unprocessed honey. The combination of honey and lemongrass makes a very tasty drink that not only helps you relax, but also helps heal.

Serves 2

1 stalk fresh lemongrass, chopped

2 cups hot water

2–4 Tbs. honey

1. Soften the lemongrass by simmering it in the water for about 20 minutes.

2. Remove from the heat and pour into a French-press coffee pot. Depress the plunger.

3. Decant the tea into teacups and add the honey to taste.

BENEFITS Honey's fructose content gives it fewer calories than cane or beet sugar and is absorbed more slowly, preventing a blood-sugar spike. Honey also has been shown to be a natural cough remedy.

Veer Photo

Immunity-Boosting Blend

This sweet, pink drink goes down easily, even when you have a tummy ache! If your strawberries aren't particularly sweet, add a teaspoon or two of honey—one of nature's antimicrobial wonders. You can use orange juice instead of carrot juice in the same amount.

Serves 2

1 cup plain low-fat yogurt

1 cup strawberries, hulls removed

¾ cup carrot juice

2 Tbs. fresh lime juice

1–2 tsp. honey (optional)

Place all the ingredients in a blender and mix for about 30 seconds or until smooth.

BENEFITS Yogurt contains probiotics, friendly bacteria that keep your intestines—a main component of your body's immune system—flourishing. Strawberries are very high in vitamin C, a known immunity booster. Limes also contain vitamin C. The carrot and orange juices provide beta-carotene, which also helps boost immunity.

 M **IB**

Banana-Mocha Smoothie

My friend and colleague Dr. Lynn Blair shared her morning smoothie recipe with me. I like it for dessert or for an afternoon pick-me-up. You can use a fresh banana if you don't have time to freeze it, decaffeinated coffee instead of regular, and skim milk instead of almond milk.

Serves 1

1 large frozen banana, cut into chunks

½ cup coffee, cooled

½ cup almond milk

¼ cup plain low-fat yogurt

¼ tsp. ground cinnamon

1 Tbs. smooth almond butter

2 Tbs. cocoa powder, divided in half

3–5 whole or crushed chocolate-covered espresso beans, as garnish

1. Place the banana chunks, coffee, almond milk, yogurt, cinnamon, almond butter, and 1 Tbs. of the cocoa powder in a blender. Whirl for 1–2 minutes or until smooth.

2. Pour into a tall glass. Top with the remaining cocoa powder and garnish with the espresso beans.

BENEFITS Cinnamon has eugenol, an anti-inflammatory that also helps keep blood sugar levels steady. The monounsaturated fats in almonds are also anti-inflammatory and heart-healthy. Coffee's polyphenols can help you focus. Yogurt contains probiotics, beneficial bacteria that keep your intestines flourishing.

extras

Pecan and Sundried Tomato Tapenade

I found the inspiration for this tapenade while at a health spa in Mexico. Of course, I put my own special FoodTrients spin on it to create a great topping for fish and a dip for crackers and bread. The pecans can be toasted or raw. I like to use sundried tomatoes preserved in olive oil.

Mix all the ingredients in a glass bowl.

CHEF'S NOTE *To make a wonderful salad dressing out of this tapenade, blend it in a food processor with up to ½ cup olive oil.*

Yields 1½ cups

½ cup olive oil

½ cup coarsely chopped pecans

½ cup minced sundried tomatoes

2–3 Tbs. sliced black olives

2 Tbs. minced cilantro leaves

2 Tbs. fresh lemon juice

1 Tbs. minced roasted garlic

1 Tbs. low-sodium soy sauce or tamari sauce

BENEFITS Pecans contain Omega-3 fatty acids, which can help improve your blood circulation by lowering triglycerides, or bad fats. Omega-3s help your skin by reducing inflammation that can lead to accelerated skin aging. Tomatoes, especially sundried, are a rich source of lycopene, an antioxidant that lowers cancer risk, protects cognitive function, and promotes prostate health.

Vegetable Crackers

These vegetable- and seed-based crackers are crunchy, hearty, and full of nutrients. Top them with cheese or enjoy them alongside soups or salads. You can use brown flaxseed meal but it will change the color of the crackers.

1. Preheat the oven to 250 degrees.

2. Soak the pumpkin seeds or pepitas in enough warm water to cover for about 1 hour, then drain.

3. Combine the seeds in a blender with the remaining ingredients and blend well for 3–5 minutes or until the mixture is very smooth. Allow to settle for 10–15 minutes.

4. Line a baking sheet with parchment paper or use a silicon baking mat. Spread the mixture evenly across the sheet until it is no thicker than ¼ inch. You should end up with a rectangle about 10 x 13 inches.

5. Bake at 250 degrees for 30 minutes.

6. Remove from the oven and cut with a pizza cutter into 2-inch squares. Reduce the oven temperature to 200 degrees and continue cooking for 1–2 hours or until the crackers are crisp but not too brown.

Yields about 24 crackers

⅓ cup pumpkin seeds (raw or toasted) or pepitas

1 cup coarsely chopped broccoli

1 cup coarsely chopped carrots

¼ cup coarsely chopped tomatoes, seeded

¼ cup golden flaxseeds

¼ tsp. sea salt

BENEFITS Broccoli contains indoles (sulfur compounds), which neutralize carcinogens and can also help reduce the adverse effects of excess estrogen. The Omega-3 fatty acids in the flaxseeds reduce inflammation and lead to beautiful, younger-looking skin.

Pico de Gallo

I like to prepare this condiment in different ways: chunky for scattering over my Mexican Chicken Lettuce Cups (page 131), and smooth as a dip for my Flaxseed and Squash Tortillas (page 241).

Combine all the ingredients in a bowl. Allow to sit for at least 10 minutes so the flavors can marry.

CHEF'S NOTE *For a chunky salsa, simply toss the ingredients together. For a dipping sauce or salsa that you can drizzle, blend the ingredients for about 30 seconds.*

Yields 2 cups

2 cups diced Roma tomatoes

¼ cup minced red onion

½ cup chopped cilantro

¼ cup fresh lemon or lime juice

1 Tbs. minced jalapeño, seedless

Salt or salt substitute and freshly ground black pepper to taste

BENEFITS Tomatoes contain lycopene, which lowers cancer risk and aids cognitive function. The indoles (sulfur compounds) in onions help neutralize carcinogens. Cilantro is a good source of vitamin K, which helps keep your bones strong.

Mom's Mayonnaise

I've been making mayonnaise at home since I was a little girl. My mother knew that homemade mayonnaise made from free-range chicken eggs tastes better than ready-made. Try flavoring your mayonnaise with 1–2 tsp. turmeric, fresh dill, pickle relish, or hot sauce for fun variations. Raw eggs, even from organic or free-range chickens, carry some risk of salmonella and should be avoided by anyone with impaired immune response.

1. In a food processor or blender, mix the egg yolks on low speed for 2 minutes.

2. With the food processor or blender still running, add the oil gradually (by the spoonful).

3. Once you have a thick, creamy mixture, add the lemon juice, garlic, and salt. Stop processing and transfer to a glass jar. Refrigerate for about an hour before use.

CHEF'S NOTE *You can use an electric mixer instead of a food processor or blender, but it will take longer to prepare.*

Yields 1 cup

2–3 egg yolks (organic, free-range, or Omega-3-enriched)

½ cup canola oil or olive oil

1 Tbs. fresh lemon juice

1 tsp. minced garlic

½ tsp. salt or salt substitute

BENEFITS Egg yolks contain choline, tryptophan, and phenylalanine for neurotransmitter production; vitamin D, which promotes calcium absorption for strong teeth and nails; and lutein, an antioxidant that reduces the risk of age-related macular degeneration and cataracts. Choline also prevents cholesterol accumulation. Eggs also provide zinc for producing collagen and elastin in skin.

Watercress Dressing

I created this dressing for my Ashitaba Potato Salad (page 87), but you can use it on just about any green leafy salad with fresh vegetables. For a thinner dressing, use regular or low-fat yogurt. Marinated or flavored, crumbled feta cheese might be fun to use in this recipe. Other nice additions would be ¼ tsp. crushed garlic and/ or ⅛ cup red onion.

Place all the ingredients in a blender and whirl together for about 30 seconds or until the watercress leaves are finely chopped.

CHEF'S NOTE *If you want to mix this by hand instead of using a blender, just chop the watercress finely and fold all the ingredients together.*

Yields 2 cups

1 cup plain Greek yogurt

1 cup whole watercress leaves, without stems

¼ cup crumbled feta cheese

½ tsp. salt or salt substitute

Dash of black or white pepper

BENEFITS Yogurt's probiotics help bolster the immune system, control inflammation, and keep the digestive process working smoothly. Watercress contains chlorophyll, which may bind to cancer-causing compounds and reduce cancer risks.

Spelt-Oat Bread

Many people suspect that modern, high-yield wheat causes digestive and health problems. I've been experimenting with ancient grains that can be used in place of regular wheat. Spelt has been grown in Germany since the Middle Ages under the name dinkel wheat. Its low-gluten content makes it easier to digest than wheat. This recipe requires white spelt flour, not whole-grain spelt flour. If modern wheat doesn't make you feel full and bloated, you can use all-purpose or bread flour instead of white spelt flour. Uncooked rolled oats give this bread additional texture.

1. Preheat the oven to 350 degrees.

2. Dissolve the yeast in warm water. When dissolved, add the sugar and salt. Set aside.

3. In a large bowl, mix the flour and oats until well blended. Arrange the mixture in a volcano shape.

4. Add the warm-water mixture and butter in the middle of the volcano. Slowly work into the flour mixture.

5. In a stand-up mixer, using the hook attachment, knead the dough for 5–8 minutes or until smooth. Set the dough in a bowl and cover it with a lightly moistened cheesecloth or towel. Let the dough rise in a warm place for about 2 hours or until it has doubled in size.

6. Punch the dough down and knead again for another 5 minutes. Set it back in the bowl and let it rise a second time for at least an hour.

7. Place the dough in a 2-lb. loaf pan or divide in half and place in two smaller loaf pans.

8. Bake at 350 degrees for 35–45 minutes or until golden brown.

Yields 1 loaf
4 tsp. rapid-rise or instant yeast
1⅓ cups warm water
5 tsp. raw sugar
1½ tsp. salt or salt substitute
4 cups light or white spelt flour
½ cup rolled oats
2 tsp. softened butter

CHEF'S NOTE *To make this loaf in a bread machine, first place the butter and water in the machine, then top with the flour mixture, using bread machine yeast. Process on the French Bread setting for about 3½ hours, then bake at 350 degrees for 35–45 minutes or until golden brown.*

BENEFITS Spelt flour has protein and fiber, which help regulate appetite and support weight loss. It also provides choline and tryptophan, nutrients used to produce good-mood neurotransmitters.

Kale-Cashew Pesto

Cashews are a sweet nut that helps to balance the sharpness of the kale. I use Tuscan kale, which is mild and tender. It's also called lacinato kale, black kale, or cavolo nero. This pesto is wonderful tossed with pasta, quinoa, or roasted potatoes or spread on sandwiches.

1. Rinse the kale in the salted water. Drain and dry with paper towels.

2. Place the kale and remaining ingredients except the cheese and 1 Tbs. of the oil into a food processor bowl. Blend for 10 seconds or until the mixture is very granular but not smooth.

3. Scrape down the sides of the bowl and add the cheese and the reserved 1 Tbs. oil. Blend for another 6–10 seconds or until you get an emerald-colored paste.

Yields 1 cup

1 cup tightly packed whole Tuscan kale leaves, without stems

2 tsp. salt in a large bowl of water for rinsing

1 cup tightly packed whole basil leaves

½ cup unsalted roasted cashews

5 Tbs. olive oil

1 tsp. crushed garlic

¼ tsp. sea salt

⅛ cup grated Parmesan cheese

BENEFITS Kale is practically a wonder drug, with all its antioxidant power from indoles (sulfur compounds), carotenoids, quercetin, vitamin C, and a bonus helping of bone-building calcium. Olive oil is rich in heart-healthy monounsaturated fats and flavonoids. Basil contains lycopene, which appears to be particularly beneficial for prostate health.

Annatto Oil and Annatto Water

Annatto seeds are native to Brazil and used in traditional Brazilian stews. In Mexico, they're called achiote seeds and are often used ground into a paste form. In America, annatto is used as a coloring agent in cheddar cheese. I use Annatto Oil to braise meats and Annatto Water in soups to add natural orange color and a slightly peppery flavor.

Annatto Oil

1. Heat the seeds and oil in a pan over low heat for about 5–7 minutes or until the oil turns a bright reddish-orange color. The seeds will sizzle and turn dark, but do not let them turn black and burn.

2. Strain to remove the seeds.

CHEF'S NOTE *You can store Annatto Oil in the refrigerator for up to a month and Annatto Water for up to a week.*

Yields ½ cup

½ cup annatto or achiote seeds (whole, not ground)

½ cup olive oil

Annatto Water

1. Add the seeds to the water and let soak for 5 minutes.

2. Work the seeds with your hands for a couple of minutes until the water turns orange.

3. Strain to remove the seeds.

Yields ½ cup

½ cup annatto or achiote seeds (whole, not ground)

½ cup warm water

BENEFITS Annatto's brilliant color comes from carotenoids, antioxidant pigments that help protect cells from ultraviolet damage. Annatto is also rich in tocotrienols, a special form of vitamin E that has cholesterol-lowering and antioxidant properties.

Flaxseed and Squash Tortillas

These tortillas are soft enough to wrap around fish but durable enough to hold fajitas. I spent weeks perfecting them! Everyone who tries them loves them. This recipe makes reddish-colored tortillas using red bell peppers, but for tortillas with green flecks use green bell peppers. I use golden flaxseeds because I prefer their color.

1. Preheat the oven to 400 degrees.

2. Roast the spaghetti squash for 30–40 minutes or until tender.

3. Scoop out 2 cups of the squash with a fork. In the bowl of a food processor, blend the squash, bell pepper, flaxseed meal, water, and salt for 3–5 minutes or until you have a thick batter.

4. Line a baking sheet with parchment paper or use a silicon baking mat. Spread the batter in 4-inch circles about ¼ inches thick.

5. Reduce the oven temperature to 225 degrees. Bake the tortillas for 1 hour or until they are slightly browned but still flexible. If they get too crispy, place them in a Ziploc bag overnight to soften them up or use them as tostadas.

Yields 6–8 tortillas

1 spaghetti squash, quartered (seeds and strings removed)

1 cup coarsely chopped red bell pepper

⅔ cup golden flaxseed meal

¼ cup water

1 tsp. salt or salt substitute

CHEF'S NOTE *If you use a different variety of squash, you might have to adjust the amount of water to achieve the right consistency. You can use regular flaxseed meal, but the tortillas will be darker when cooked.*

BENEFITS Flaxseed contains fiber and Omega-3 fatty acids, which can lower cholesterol and reduce your risk of heart disease, and vitamin E, which protects the heart and the skin from the sun's aging effects. The carotenoids in squash and peppers are precursors to vitamin A, which boosts immunity and helps keep eyes healthy.

Macadamia Cream and Mock Sour Cream

This rich, satisfying, heart-healthy version of cream is made with soaked macadamia nuts. You won't believe how good it is.

Macadamia Cream

1. Soak the nuts in the water for 1 hour.
2. Blend in a powerful blender or food processor for 1–2 minutes or until the cream is thick, smooth, and somewhat fluffy.

Yields 2 cups

1 cup raw, organic macadamia nuts

1 cup warm water

Mock Sour Cream

1. Combine the lemon juice and ½ cup of the Macadamia Cream.
2. Mix in the remaining Macadamia Cream.

Yields 2 cups

1 Tbs. fresh lemon juice

1 recipe Macadamia Cream, divided in half

BENEFITS Macadamia nuts are very heart healthy thanks to their monounsaturated fats and choline, which help prevent cholesterol accumulation. The vitamin E in the nuts also reduces your risk of heart disease. These nuts are also a good source of iron, which delivers oxygen to cells and muscles and keeps you energized.

Homemade Chicken Stock

There's no substitute for homemade chicken stock. It's easy to make and freezes very well. I use this stock in my Chicken Soup with Coconut Meat (page 69) and my Chicken Lentil Soup (page 73). You can add 1 Tbs. of any fresh herb to this recipe with the parsley, depending on the flavor you want. Rosemary, thyme, oregano, and tarragon work well. You can even add some lavender and/or lemon zest.

1. In a covered stockpot, boil all the ingredients except the parsley for 30–40 minutes or until the chicken is cooked through.

2. Add the parsley and simmer, uncovered, for another 10 minutes.

3. Allow the soup to cool a bit, then strain it.

4. To reduce the fat content, place the stock in the refrigerator overnight. The fat will rise to the top and harden. Skim it out and discard.

5. Discard the vegetables, bones, and skin and reserve the chicken meat for another use.

Yields 3 cups

4 cups water

1 free-range or organic chicken, cut into 6–8 pieces

1 cup diced carrots

1 cup chopped celery

1 cup chopped onion

1 Tbs. chopped ginger

1 Tbs. chopped garlic

1 tsp. sea salt

¼ tsp. white pepper

½ cup chopped parsley

BENEFITS Chicken stock made from raw bones is high in collagen, hyaluronic acid, chondroitin and other glycosamino glycans—nutrients that can help strengthen joints and plump the skin. Garlic and onions boost immunity through allicin and quercetin, respectively.

Homemade Vegetable Stock

Vegetable stock is a flavorful, fat-free, vegan base for healthy cooking. I like to use it for my soups and sauces, especially if I'm feeding vegetarian friends or trying to avoid animal fats (see my White Bean Soup, page 71). Making the stock myself gives me lots of room to use seasonal vegetables. And since the stock is strained after cooking, I can use the stems and stalks of the vegetables, reserving the best parts for other dishes. You can add other vegetables, too, such as carrots, fennel, or kale.

1. Heat the oil in a large stockpot with a heavy bottom. Cook the onion and garlic over medium heat for 1 minute.

2. Add the zucchini, celery, and broccoli and cook for 10 minutes.

3. Add the water, parsley, and herb seasoning and boil for 30 minutes.

4. Allow the stock to cool. Strain and season with the salt and pepper.

Yields 3 cups

1 Tbs. olive oil

½ cup chopped white onion

1 Tbs. crushed garlic

1 cup chopped zucchini

1 cup chopped celery

½ cup chopped broccoli

4 cups water

¼ cup chopped parsley

1 Tbs. Italian herb seasoning

1 tsp. sea salt

¼ tsp. white pepper

BENEFITS Vegetables are a mainstay of a healthy diet. Although cooking and straining vegetables removes many nutrients, this homemade stock remains a flavorful, fat-free, vegan base for healthy cooking.

Chicken Gravy

I created this gravy to go with my Chicken Meatloaf (page 125), but it's just as wonderful over roasted chicken or turkey. My Greek friends add ¼ cup fresh lemon juice and 1 Tbs. minced garlic. You can use spelt flour or flour from hard red wheat and store-bought chicken broth instead of homemade. Throwing in some minced parsley after cooking adds flavor, texture, and nutrients. This gravy is pure comfort food, but I consider it an allowable indulgence in the context of a nutritious diet.

1. In a saucepan, melt the butter and add the flour.
2. Cook over medium heat for 5 minutes, stirring continuously, or until the flour turns light brown.
3. Gradually add the chicken stock ½ cup at a time, whisking to remove lumps, for about 10 minutes.
4. Add the Worcestershire and soy sauces and continue stirring for 5–10 minutes or until the gravy thickens.

CHEF'S NOTE *To give this gravy some zing, add about ½ cup of sherry wine. Leave out the Worcestershire sauce and use 1 tsp. salt or salt substitute instead of the soy sauce.*

Yields 2 cups

4 Tbs. butter

3 Tbs. white or whole-wheat flour

2 cups Homemade Chicken Stock (page 244) or store-bought

2 Tbs. Lea & Perrins Worcestershire sauce

1 Tbs. low-sodium soy sauce

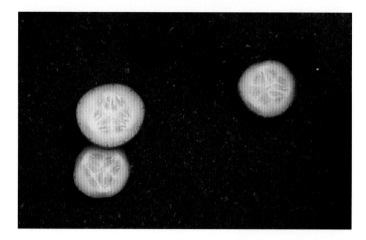

Avocado-Cucumber Dip and Dressing

This dip or dressing gets its creamy consistency and full body from blended pine nuts and avocado and its beauty benefits from avocados, pine nuts, and cucumbers. I use roasted garlic in this recipe because raw garlic is too harsh. If you don't have roasted garlic on hand, you can use garlic powder or bottled chopped garlic.

1. Soak the pine nuts in enough warm water to cover for 1 hour. Drain and set aside.

2. In a blender or food processor, whirl the cucumber, and celery 1–3 minutes or until liquefied.

3. Add the pine nuts and blend 1–2 minutes.

4. Add the remaining ingredients and blend 1–2 minutes or until the mixture is smooth and creamy.

Yields 2 cups

½ cup raw pine nuts

½ cup peeled, seeded, and chopped cucumber

¼ cup chopped celery

½ cup avocado

¼ cup chopped onion

1–2 Tbs. fresh lemon juice

½ tsp. roasted garlic

½ tsp. sea salt

BENEFITS Both avocados and nuts contain monounsaturated fats, which help lower bad cholesterol and reduce the risk of heart attack and stroke. Cucumbers are a good source of vitamin K, which contributes to strong bones. They are also great natural hydrators, helping skin to stay fresh and youthful looking.

Thinkstock Photo by ChamilleWhite

FoodTrients® Dessert Spice Mix

I love the idea of being able to shake more anti-aging ingredients into my food from a spice jar. This unsweetened mix can be added to brownies or cakes or even a Mexican molé sauce to contribute extra flavor and antioxidants. If you're watching your caffeine intake, you can use decaffeinated coffee.

Place all the ingredients in a jar and shake well.

Yields ⅓ cup

8 tsp. unsweetened cocoa powder

4 tsp. instant coffee

2 tsp. cinnamon

1 tsp. ground cardamom (brown, not green)

1 tsp. ground nutmeg

BENEFITS The catechins and flavonoids found in cocoa reduce your risk of heart disease and heart attack. Coffee contains polyphenols, which help prevent damage to your DNA. The eugenol in cinnamon is an anti-inflammatory that helps stabilize blood sugar. The cineole in cardamom is also an anti-inflammatory.

part 3
RESOURCES

Menus for Entertaining

These menus work best as a buffet meal with multiple entrees where guests can pick and choose their favorites.

Breakfast / Brunch

Mind and Beauty Juice
Melon Balls with Mint and Prosciutto
Exotic Fruit Salad with Yogurt and Granola
Quinoa Porridge
Salmon with Ginger-Apricot Sauce (chilled)
Citrusy Asparagus
Stuffed Peaches
Sweet Mung Beans

Mexican / Southwestern

Guacamole with Pomegranate Seeds
Black Bean Salad
Turkey Molé
Grilled Fish Tacos
Chicken Fajitas
Rice and Corn Pudding

Spanish / South American

Crab-Mango Cocktail
Chilled Cucumber Soup
Seafood Chowder
Crock-Pot Chicken with Annatto
Poached Cod à la Française
Vegetarian Stir-Fry Noodles with Annatto
Macadamia-Cream Flan

Middle-Eastern

Annatto Hummus
Olive and Watercress Tapenade
Couscous Salad
Rack of Lamb with Fig Marinade
Flaxseed-Crusted Tuna
Wild Boar Kebabs
Cauliflower Steaks with Herbed Goat Cheese
Spiced Nuts
Strawberry-Banana Sorbet

Vegan

Cashew and Avocado Dip
Shirataki Noodle Salad
White Bean Soup
Vegan Mac and Cheese
Lemon Garlic Pasta
Garlicky Green Beans
Raspberry-Cream Banana Splits
Dark Chocolate Mousse

Gluten-Free

Mangosteen Chutney
Stir-Fry Korean Glass Noodles
   (made with tamari sauce)
Chicken Soup with Coconut Meat
Asian Fusion Shrimp and Quinoa
Beef on a Salt Block
Squab Stuffed with Red Rice
Atchara Pickle
Stuffed Sugar Pumpkins
Jujube Crumble
Seasonal Fruit Upside-Down Cake

Kid-Friendly

Egg Salad with Turmeric
Asian Chicken Salad
Roasted Eggplant and Pepperoni Pizza
Orange Tomato Soup
Super Grilled Cheese Sandwiches
Baby Back Ribs with Baobab Sauce
Coconut-Lemongrass Rice
Mini Cheddar-Rice Cupcakes
Baobab Butter Squares

Guide to Age-Defying FoodTrients®

FoodTrient	Potential Benefits
Allicin	Reduces risk of heart disease. heart attack, stroke, cancer.
Anthocyanins	Reduces risk of cancer.
Carotenoids	Reduces risk of heart disease and certain cancers. Supports immune function.
Catechins	Reduces risk of heart disease, heart attack. Protects against certain cancers. Helps prevent dental cavities. May enhance weight loss.
Chlorophyll	Protects against certain cancers.
Choline	Supports healthy brain function and memory. Protects liver. Prevents cholesterol accumulation.
Curcumin	Reduces risk of heart disease, inflammatory conditions, and certain cancers.
Fiber	Reduces risk of heart disease and certain cancers. Aids with appetite. control and weight management. Helps prevent constipation. Helps stabilize blood sugar.

Primary Sources	Properties*			
Fresh garlic	Anti-inflammatory Disease Prevention	Ai	DP	
Blue, purple, or red fruits and vegetables (esp. berries, grapes, and eggplants)	Disease Prevention	DP		
Orange vegetables (esp. carrots, pumpkin, sweet potato, winter squash)	Antioxidant Disease Prevention Immunity Booster	Ao DP IB		
Berries, chocolate, grapes, tea	Disease Prevention Beauty Weight Loss	DP	B	WL
Parsley, spinach, watercress, wheatgrass	Antioxidant Disease Prevention	Ao DP		
Egg yolks, liver, wheat germ	Disease Prevention Mind	DP	M	
Curry powder, turmeric	Anti-inflammatory Antioxidant Disease Prevention	Ai Ao DP		
Fruits, legumes, vegetables, whole grains	Disease Prevention Weight Loss	DP		WL

Guide to Age-Defying FoodTrients®

FoodTrient	Potential Benefits
Gingerol	Alleviates nausea and inflammatory conditions. Reduces risk of certain cancers.
Indoles	Reduces risk of certain cancers.
Isoflavones	Increases bone density. Reduces risk of cancer and heart disease.
Isothiocyanates	Reduces risk of certain cancers.
Lauric acid	Improves cholesterol balance, prostate health.
Lutein	Reduces risk of age-related macular degeneration and cataracts.
Lycopene	Reduces risk of certain cancers, including lung and prostate.
Oleocanthal/oleuropein	Reduces risk of heart disease, inflammatory disorders.

Primary Sources	Properties*			
Ginger	Anti-inflammatory Disease Prevention	Ai	DP	
Cruciferous vegetables (esp. broccoli, Brussels sprouts, cabbage)	Disease Prevention		DP	
Edamame (soybeans), miso, soy milk, soy sauce, tempeh, tofu	Disease Prevention Strength		DP	S
Cruciferous vegetables (esp. Brussels sprouts, kale, mustard and turnip greens), horseradish, wasabe	Disease Prevention		DP	
Coconut milk, coconut oil	Anti-inflammatory Disease Prevention	Ai	DP	
Leafy greens (e.g., kale, spinach, collards, and turnip greens)	Antioxidant Disease Prevention	Ao	DP	
Guava, pink and red grapefruit, tomato products, watermelon	Antioxidant Disease Prevention	Ao	DP	
Olive oil	Anti-inflammatory Antioxidant Disease Prevention	Ai Ao	DP	

Guide to Age-Defying FoodTrients®

FoodTrient	Potential Benefits
Omega-3 fatty acids	Reduces risk of heart disease. Protects against sun damage and skin aging. Protects against dementia.
Potassium	Reduces risk of stroke, osteoporosis, kidney stones.
Probiotics	Increases resistance to colds and flu. Protects against food-borne illness and inflammatory disorders. Helps prevent constipation.
Quercetin	Reduces inflammation. May reduce allergic sensitivity.
Resveratrol	Reduces risk of heart disease and cancer.
Selenium	Reduces risk of cancer. Increases resistance to infection.
Sulfur compounds	Reduces risk of heart disease and cancer. Supports joints and connective tissue.
Vitamin C	Increases resistance to infection. Reduces risk of cancer, stroke, and cataracts. Protects against sun damage and skin aging.

Primary Sources	Properties*				
Fish, flaxseed, walnuts	Anti-inflammatory Disease Prevention Mind, Beauty	Ai	DP	M B	
Acorn squash, bananas, lima beans, potatoes, prunes, spinach	Disease Prevention Strength		DP		S
Kefir, unpasteurized sauerkraut, yogurt	Anti-inflammatory Immunity Booster	Ai	IB		
Onions, apples, broccoli, citrus, kale, onions	Anti-inflammatory	Ai			
Cranberries, grapes, grape juice, peanuts, red wine, red wine vinegar	Anti-inflammatory Disease Prevention	Ai	DP		
Brazil nuts, mushrooms, poultry, seafood	Antioxidant Disease Prevention Immunity Booster	Ao DP IB			
Garlic, leeks, onions	Anti-inflammatory Disease Prevention Strength	Ai	DP		S
Berries, citrus, dark green veggies, melons, red peppers	Anti-inflammatory Antioxidant Disease Prevention Immunity Booster Beauty	Ai Ao DP IB		B	

Guide to Age-Defying FoodTrients®

FoodTrient	Potential Benefits
Vitamin E	Reduces risk of heart disease. Increases resistance to infection. Protects against sun damage and skin aging. Supports healthy brain function.
Zinc	Increases resistance to infection. Reduces risk of macular degeneration.

Primary Sources	Properties*		
Nuts, vegetable oils, whole grains	Anti-inflammatory Antioxidant Disease Prevention Mind Beauty	**Ai** **Ao** **DP**	**M** **B**
Beef, legumes, nuts, shellfish	Disease Prevention Immunity Booster	**DP** **IB**	

*FoodTrient Properties and Their Icons

Ai Anti-Inflammatory: Reduces the inflammation process in cells, tissues, and blood vessels, helping to slow aging and lower the risk of long-term disease.

Ao Antioxidant: Prevents and repairs oxidative damage to cells caused by free radicals.

DP Disease Prevention: Reduces risk factors for common degenerative and age-related diseases (like cancer and diabetes).

IB Immunity Booster (including Anti-Bacterial): Supports the body's resistance to infection and strengthens immune vigilance and response.

M Mind: Improves mood, memory, and focus.

B Beauty: Promotes vibrant skin and hair and helps keep eyes healthy.

S Strength: Builds strength for bones, muscles and joints. Increases bone density, builds and repairs tissue.

WL Weight Loss: Encourages improved metabolism and digestion.

Sources: USDA Agricultural Research Service Nutrient Data Laboratory; Linus Pauling Micronutrient Information Center (Oregon State University); U.S. Department of Health and Human Services

Guide to Recipe Benefits

ANTI-INFLAMMATORY	ANTIOXIDANT	DISEASE PREVENTION	IMMUNITY BOOSTER	MIND	BEAUTY	STRENGTH	WEIGHT LOSS		
								APPETIZERS	
			■		■			Crab-Mango Cocktail	45
■					■			Guacamole with Pomegranate Seeds	47
■		■						Olive and Watercress Tapenade	49
■			■					Mangosteen Chutney	51
■	■				■			Melon Balls with Mint and Prosciutto	53
	■	■						Vegetable Chips	55
■	■				■			Annatto Hummus	57
■				■	■			Spiced Nuts	59
■		■						Cashew and Avocado Dip	61
	■		■					Stir-Fry Korean Glass Noodles	63
								SOUPS	
	■				■			"Cream" of Broccoli Soup	67
						■	■	Chicken Soup with Coconut Meat	69
	■						■	White Bean Soup	71
						■	■	Chicken Lentil Soup	73
	■				■			Minestrone-Style Soup	75
■				■	■			Seafood Chowder	77
	■							Orange Tomato Soup	79
				■	■			Chilled Cucumber Soup	80
								SALADS	
					■	■	■	Black Bean Salad	83
		■	■		■			Asian Chicken Salad	85
		■			■			Ashitaba Potato Salad	87
				■	■			Egg Salad with Turmeric	89
■	■		■					Exotic Fruit Salad with Yogurt and Granola	91
		■			■		■	Shirataki Noodle Salad	93
		■			■			Arugula and Radicchio Salad	95
	■	■			■			Shrimp and Grapefruit Salad	97
						■	■	Seaweed Salad	99
		■			■			Couscous Salad	101
			■		■		■	Wild Rice and Quinoa Salad	103
■								Curried Chicken Salad	104

ANTI-INFLAMMATORY	ANTIOXIDANT	DISEASE PREVENTION	IMMUNITY BOOSTER	MIND	BEAUTY	STRENGTH	WEIGHT LOSS	MAIN COURSES	
								Vegetable	
	■				■			Vegetarian Stir-Fry Noodles with Annatto	107
■				■	■			Roasted Eggplant and Pepperoni Pizza	109
					■	■		Super Grilled Cheese Sandwiches	111
				■				Vegan Mac and Cheese	113
■				■			■	Quinoa Porridge	115
		■			■			Lemon Garlic Pasta	117
								Poultry	
■				■				Chicken Curry with Moringa	119
					■	■		Crock-Pot Chicken with Annatto	121
				■		■		Beer-Basted Chicken	123
				■		■		Chicken Meatloaf	125
			■			■		Chicken Fajitas	127
				■		■		Roasted Chicken	129
		■			■			Mexican Chicken Lettuce Cups	131
			■	■				Turkey Molé	133
				■		■		Squab Stuffed with Red Rice	135
■						■		Quail Adobo	137
								Meat	
				■		■		Wild Boar Kebabs	139
■	■					■		Buffalo Sliders	141
		■			■			Ostrich Meatballs	143
■			■				■	Chia Fettuccine with Southwestern Pork and Vegetables	145
		■			■	■		Roasted Pork Shoulder	147
				■		■		Rack of Lamb with Fig Marinade	149
	■	■				■		Baby Back Ribs with Baobab Sauce	151
						■		Beef on a Salt Block	153

continued on next page

Guide to Recipe Benefits

Anti-Inflammatory	Antioxidant	Disease Prevention	Immunity Booster	Mind	Beauty	Strength	Weight Loss		
								MAIN COURSES continued	
								Seafood	
▪				▪	▪			Salmon Poached in Pickling Spices	155
	▪						▪	Asian Fusion Shrimp and Quinoa	157
▪				▪	▪			Sardine Wrap	159
▪		▪		▪				Grilled Fish Tacos	161
▪				▪	▪			Flaxseed-Crusted Tuna	163
▪				▪	▪			Salmon with Ginger-Apricot Sauce	165
▪				▪				Poached Cod à la Française	166
								SIDES	
	▪				▪			Baby Bok Choy	169
	▪				▪			Garlicky Green Beans	171
▪						▪		Celery Root Mashed Potatoes	173
	▪		■					Swiss Chard and Kale Combo	175
	▪				▪			Weller Red Cabbage	177
▪	▪							Tropical Yams	179
	▪						▪	Atchara Pickle	181
	▪							Citrusy Asparagus	183
	▪		■					Mushroom Medley	185
	■				▪			Stuffed Sugar Pumpkins	187
	▪				▪			Cauliflower Steaks with Herbed Goat Cheese	189
▪	▪		■					Coconut-Lemongrass Rice	190
								DESSERTS	
▪			■		▪			Raspberry-Cream Banana Splits	193
			■	▪				Jujube Crumble	195
	▪					▪		Sweet Mung Beans	197
▪	■				▪			Stuffed Peaches	199
▪	■							Banana Citrus Cake	201
					▪	▪		Mini Cheddar-Rice Cupcakes	203
	■	▪						Baobab Butter Squares	205
▪				▪				Rice and Corn Pudding	207
				▪	▪			Macadamia Cream Flan	209

ANTI-INFLAMMATORY	ANTIOXIDANT	DISEASE PREVENTION	IMMUNITY BOOSTER	MIND	BEAUTY	STRENGTH	WEIGHT LOSS		
								DESSERTS continued	
			■					Strawberry-Banana Sorbet	211
	■	■						Coconut-Rice Cake	213
		■						Dark Chocolate Mousse	215
		■			■			Moringa Chiffon Muffins	217
				■	■			Seasonal Fruit Upside-Down Cake	219
								DRINKS	
■				■		■		Coconut Slushie	222
	■			■				Jujube Tea	223
		■	■					Beet, Orange, and Watercress Juice	224
■	■	■	■					Mind and Beauty Juice	225
			■	■				Honey-Lemongrass Tea	226
■	■	■	■	■				Immunity-Boosting Blend	227
			■	■				Banana-Mocha Smoothie	228
								EXTRAS	
■				■	■			Pecan and Sundried Tomato Tapenade	231
		■			■			Vegetable Crackers	232
		■	■					Pico de Gallo	233
				■	■			Mom's Mayonnaise	235
		■	■					Watercress Dressing	236
				■	■	■		Spelt-Oat Bread	237
	■	■						Kale-Cashew Pesto	239
■		■			■			Annatto Oil	240
■		■			■			Annatto Water	240
■					■			Flaxseed and Squash Tortillas	241
■								Macadamia Cream	243
■								Mock Sour Cream	243
			■			■		Homemade Chicken Stock	244
		■	■					Homemade Vegetable Stock	245
				■		■		Chicken Gravy	246
■					■			Avocado Cucumber Dip and Dressing	247
■	■			■				FoodTrients® Dessert Spice Mix	248

Sugar Substitutes

Agave Nectar

1 cup sugar: ⅔ cup agave nectar

Chef's Note: Reduce recipe liquid by 2 Tbs.; reduce oven temperature by 25 degrees.

Barley-malt Syrup

1 cup sugar: 1¼ cups barely-malt syrup

Chef's Note: Reduce recipe liquid by 2–3 Tbs.; add ⅟₁₆ tsp. baking soda for baked goods.

Brown-rice Syrup

1 cup sugar: 1¼ cups brown-rice syrup

Chef's Note: Reduce recipe liquid by 2–3 Tbs.; add ⅟₁₆ tsp. baking soda for baked goods.

Coconut Sugar

1 cup sugar: ⅔ cup coconut sugar

Chef's Note: Cover mixing bowl with a towel when beating to avoid sugar dust coating the kitchen.

Date Sugar

1 cup sugar: ⅔ cup date sugar

Chef's Note: Cover mixing bowl with a towel when beating to avoid sugar dust coating the kitchen.

Erythritol

1 tsp. sugar: 1 tsp. plus erythritol

1 Tbs. sugar: 1 Tbs. plus erythritol

1 cup sugar: 1–1½ cups erythritol

Chef's Note: Erythritol is about 60–80 percent as sweet as sugar so you many want to add more of it to achieve the same sweetness.

Maple Syrup

1 cup sugar: ¾ cup maple sugar

Chef's Note: Reduce recipe liquid by ¼ cup; add ⅛ tsp. baking soda.

Stevia

1 tsp. sugar: a pinch of stevia powdered extract, 2–4 drops of stevia liquid extract

1 Tbs. sugar: ¼ tsp. of stevia powdered extract, 6–9 drops of stevia liquid extract

1 cup sugar: 1 tsp. of stevia powdered extract, 1 tsp. stevia liquid extract

Chef's Note: Stevia does not work well by itself in baked goods because it changes the texture. You can substitute part of the sugar, erythritol, or xylitol with stevia, however.

Xylitol

1 cup sugar: 1 cup xylitol

Chef's Note: Start by substituting only part of the sugar; watch for digestive upset.

Truvia

1 tsp. sugar: ¼ tsp. (½ packet)

1 Tbs. sugar: 1¼ tsp. (1½ packets)

⅓ cup sugar: 2 Tbs. plus 1 tsp. (8 packets)

¼ cup sugar: 1 Tbs. plus 2 tsp. (6 packets)

1 cup sugar: ⅓ cup plus 1½ Tbs. (24 packets)

Chef's Note: Truvia is a zero-calorie sweetener made from the leaves of the stevia plant. The company also has a baking product that combines sugar and stevia.

Useful Equivalents and Metric Conversions

Cooking Measurements

16 tablespoons	=	1 cup
12 tablespoons	=	¾ cup
10 tablespoons + 2 teaspoons	=	⅔ cup
8 tablespoons	=	½ cup
6 tablespoons	=	⅜ cup
5 tablespoons + 1 teaspoon	=	⅓ cup
4 tablespoons	=	¼ cup
2 tablespoons + 2 teaspoons	=	⅙ cup
2 tablespoons	=	⅛ cup
1 tablespoon	=	1/16 cup
2 cups	=	1 pint
2 pints	=	1 quart
3 teaspoons	=	1 tablespoon
48 teaspoons	=	1 cup

Oven Temperatures

250° F = 120° C

275° F = 135° C

300° F = 150° C

325° F = 160° C

350° F = 180° C

375° F = 190° C

400° F = 200° C

425° F = 220° C

450° F = 230° C

475° F = 245° C

500° F = 260° C

Conversion Table for Cooking

⅛ teaspoon	=	0.5 milliliter
⅕ teaspoon	=	1 milliliter
¼ teaspoon	=	1.25 milliliters
½ teaspoon	=	2.5 milliliters
¾ teaspoon	=	3.7 milliliters
1 teaspoon	=	5 milliliters
1¼ teaspoons	=	6.16 milliliters
1½ teaspoons	=	7.5 milliliters
1¾ teaspoons	=	8.63 milliliters
2 teaspoons	=	10 milliliters
1 tablespoon (1/16 cup)	=	15 milliliters
2 tablespoons (⅛ cup)	=	29.5 milliliters
⅕ cup	=	47 milliliters
¼ cup (4 tablespoons)	=	59 milliliters
½ cup	=	118.3 milliliters
1 cup	=	237 milliliters
2 cups or 1 pint	=	473 milliliters
3 cups	=	710 milliliters
4 cups or 1 quart	=	.95 liters
4 quarts or 1 gallon	=	3.8 liters
1 fluid oz.	=	30 milliliters (28 grams)
1 pound	=	454 grams

Guide to Ingredients

Ingredient	Recipe	Sources
Agar-agar powder	Sweet Mung Beans	Online sources such as Amazon.com, Barryfarm.com, iHerb.com
Agar-agar bar		Eden Organic: Edenfoods.com/store/ product_info.php?products_id=108960
Annatto or achiote seeds	Annatto Oil Annatto Water	Hispanic markets; Penzeys: Penzeys.com
Ashitaba plant	Sardine Wrap	Etsy.com; Plant Delights Nursery: plant delights.com/ Angelica-keiskei-for-sale/Buy-Ashitaba/
Ashitaba seeds	Ashitaba Potato Salad	Horizon Herbs: Horizonherbs.com/ product.asp?specific=1302
Baobab powder	Baby Back Ribs with Baobab Sauce Baobab Butter Squares	Baobab Foods: Baobest baobab: Amazon.com; Baobabfoods.myshopify.com
Chia pasta	Chia Fettuccine with Southwestern Pork and Vegetables	BonaChia: Aldentepasta.com/product-categories/bonachia
Bragg Liquid Aminos	Vegetarian Stir-Fry Noodles with Annatto	Bragg: Bragg.com
Candied (crystallized) ginger	Ginger Tea	Asian or Middle Eastern markets
Coconut cream	Rasberry-Cream Banana Splits Rice and Corn Pudding	Trader Joe's market
Coconut meat (raw and frozen)	Crab-Mango Cocktail Coconut Slushie	Asian and specialty markets; Exotic Superfoods: Exoticsuperfoods.com/collections/ coconut/products/young-thai-coconut-meat
Couscous (golden, natural, tricolor, whole-wheat)	Couscous Salad	Grocery stores; Bob's Red Mill: Bobsredmill.com/ search.php?mode=search&page=1
Frozen seafood blend	Seafood Chowder	Trader Joe's market
Golden flaxseed meal	Flaxseed and Squash Tortillas	Bob's Red Mill: Bobsredmill.com/ golden-flaxseed-meal.html
Goji berries	Curried Chicken Salad	Melissa's: Melissas.com
Jujubes	Exotic Fruit Salad with Yogurt and Granola Jujube Crumble Jujube Tea	Melissa's: Melissas.com

Ingredient	Recipe	Sources
Himalayan salt blocks	Beef on a Salt Block	Kitchen stores and food shops (e.g., Crate and Barrel, Sur la Table, WilliamsSonoma); SaltWorks: saltworks.us
Korean glass noodles	Stir-Fry Korean Glass Noodles	Asian markets
Lemon garlic pasta	Lemon Garlic Pasta	Pappardelle Pasta: Pappardellespasta.com/products/ dried-pasta/flat-cut-pasta
Lemongrass (fresh) Lemongrass (stir-in paste)	Coconut-Lemongrass Rice	Indian and Asian markets; Melissa's: Melissas.com; Gourmet Garden: Gourmetgarden.com/en/product/ 106/lemongrass-stir-paste
Mangosteens	Mangosteen Chutney	Exotic fruit purveyors; Melissa's: Melissas.com
Mochiko	Coconut-Rice Cake	Bob's Red Mill: Bobsredmill.com/ sweet-white-rice-flour.html
Moringa powder	Chicken Curry with Moringa Moringa Chiffon Muffins	Moringa for Life: Moringaforlife.com/products/ bulk-moringa-leaf-powder
Quinoa Red quinoa	Asian Fusion Shrimp Quinoa Porridge	Grocery stores; Roland Food: Rolandfood.elsstore.com Bob's Red Mill: Bobsredmill.com/ product.php?productid=1115&cat=&page=1
Pickling salts kit	Salmon Poached in Pickling Spices	The Grommet:Thegrommet.com/food-drink/ backyard-farmer-pickling-kit
Pomegranate molasses	Arugula and Radicchio Salad	Middle Eastern markets; Surfas: Culinarydistrict.com/ 5122.html
Rice noodles	Vegetarian Stir-Fry Noodles with Annatto	Grocery stores; Thai Kitchen: Thaikitchen.elsstore.com
Seaweed Organic Irish seaweed Organic Japanese seaweed Nori seaweed	Seaweed Salad	Whole Foods Market; Asian markets AlgAran Seaweed Products: Seaweedproducts.ie/ OrganicIrishSeavegEdibleSeaweed.htm Eden Organic: Edenfoods.com/store/ product_info.php?products_id=108900 Grocery stores
Shirataki noodles	Shirataki Noodle Salad	Asian markets; Skinny Dip: Skinnydipnoodles.com
Sun-dried golden berries	Wild Rice and Quinoa Salad	Navitas Naturals: navitasnaturals.com/product/ 45Goldenberries.html
White (or light) spelt flour	Spelt-Oat Bread	Bob's Red Mill: Bobsredmill.com/light-spelt-flours.html

Index

About the Author

Photograph by Gary Moss

Grace O, author of *The Age GRACEfully Cookbook: The Power of FoodTrients to Promote Health and Well-Being for a Joyful and Sustainable Life,* has been cooking and baking professionally and recreationally all of her adult life. As a child in Southeast Asia, she learned the culinary arts by her mother's side in her family's cooking school. She became so well versed in hospitality and the culinary arts, she eventually took over the cooking school and opened three restaurants. She is widely credited with popularizing shrimp on sugarcane skewers and being one of the first culinarians to make tapas a global trend. She has cooked for ruling families and royalty.

Grace O's move to America precipitated a career in health care, inspired by her father, who was a physician. Twenty years and much hard work later, she operates skilled nursing facilities in California.

Grace O strives to create flavorful food using the finest ingredients that ultimately lead to good health. Her recipes, although low in saturated fat, salt, and sugar, are high in flavor. Grace employs spices from all over the world to enliven her dishes, creating food that is different and delicious. She believes that food can be just as effective at fighting aging as the most expensive skin creams. And since she's over 50 herself, she's living proof of that theory.

Her first cookbook, *The Age GRACEfully Cookbook,* won the Gold Award in the 5th Annual Living Now Book Awards. Grace O's blog, *Aging Gracefully,* appears weekly on FoodTrients.com. She is also a regular contributor to ScrubsMag.com, the award-winning lifestyle nursing magazine and website, and is a bimonthly columnist for the *Asian Journal* newspaper.